Instructor's Manual and Test Bank for

Social Gerontology
A Multidisciplinary Perspective

Fifth Edition

Nancy Hooyman
School of Social Work
University of Washington

H. Asuman Kiyak
Institute on Aging
University of Washington

Allyn and Bacon
Boston • London • Toronto • Sydney • Tokyo • Singapore

INSTRUCTORS MANUAL

TABLE OF CONTENTS

Page

To The Instructor:

This "Instructor's Manual" is intended to assist you in designing your lesson plans and lectures for topics covered in the fifth edition of our textbook "Social Gerontology: A Multidisciplinary Perspective." A glossary of key terms and concepts has been developed for each chapter of this manual, identical to the glossary at the end of each chapter in the textbook. In addition, several discussion topics have been included for each chapter to aid you in generating class discussion and essay questions for examinations. A series of multiple choice and true/false questions are also included for each chapter. These questions focus on the key concepts presented in the book. You will also find a Resource Directory of organizations, periodicals, and newsletters in the field of gerontology at the end of this manual. To the extent possible, we have included Web Sites for these organizations and periodical publishers.

We hope you will find the "Instructor's Manual" to be a useful adjunct to the textbook and in teaching social gerontology. We are indebted to Ms. Carol Dean, who has worked diligently to update the resource directory, and to revise the test bank for this edition.

NRH
HAK

CHAPTER 1: THE GROWTH OF SOCIAL GERONTOLOGY

Glossary

Active vs. Dependent Life Expectancy
Ageism
Baltimore Longitudinal Study of Aging
Cohort
Competence Model
Compression of Morbidity
Cross Sectional Research
Environmental Press

Geriatrics
Gerontology
Life Expectancy
Longitudinal Research
Maximum Life Span
Person-Environment Perspective
Sequential Research Designs

Topics for Discussion

1.   Distinguish between different types of aging. To what extent would one expect consistency among these types of aging?

2.   What historical and cultural factors have differentially influenced the cohort of people who are currently aged 65 to 75 and those aged 35 to 45?

3.   Distinguish among the young-old, the old-old, and the oldest-old in terms of social and health characteristics.

4.   Discuss the benefits of studying social gerontology from a dynamic person-environment transactional perspective.

5.   Discuss your own reasons for learning about older adults and the aging process, and the benefits you expect to gain from your learning process.

6.   Discuss the influence of mortality and birthrates, as well as life expectancy, on the significant increase observed in the older population today.

7.   What are the economic, political, and social implications of the increasing rectangularization of the population pyramid?

8.   Discuss the geographic distribution of the older US population and implications for policies in states with higher and lower than average proportions of older persons in their population.

9.   What are some reasons for the growth of the older population in developing countries?

10.   Describe some alternatives to the hypothesis of compressed morbidity for future cohorts of elderly persons.

11.   Compare your own experiences as members of a birth cohort with those from the cohorts of the 1920's and 1930's.

12.   Describe the age/period/cohort problem in social gerontological research. What research designs have been developed to overcome some of these problems? What are the strengths and weaknesses of each design?

13.   Discuss the advantages and disadvantages of conducting longitudinal research in aging.

14.   Discuss the strengths and weaknesses of existing measures of stereotypes toward aging and older adults.

Multiple Choice

(E) 1.   Which of the following is the poorest definition of age from a developmental perspective?
   a.   biological age
X   b.   chronological age
   c.   sociocultural age
   d.   psychological age

(M) 2.   Mary is 60 years old, drives a Corvette, and has a teenage daughter. She would be considered to have a young:
   a.   biological age
   b.   chronological age
   c.   sociocultural age
X   d.   psychological age

(M) 3.   In terms of psychological age, which of the following people is the youngest?

   a.   Michelle, a college graduate at age 17
   b.   Anne, a secretary at age 25
   c.   Sarah, a school teacher at age 55
X   d.   Cathy, a college sophomore at age 48

(E) 4.   There are approximately _____ older adults in the US today.

X   a.   34,000,000
   b.   3,000,000
   c.   20,000,000
   d.   3,300,000

(M) 5.   In the United States, by the year 2030 the number of people over 65+:

   a.   will finally be less than the number of adolescents
   b.   be identical to the number of middle-aged adults
   c.   will have declined substantially from current levels
X   d.   will be about the same as the number of children

(E) 6.   Which of the following groups comprise the fastest growing segment of the US population?
   a.   white children
X   b.   people aged 85+
   c.   immigrants
   d.   blue-collar workers

(E) 7. Gerontology is the field of study that examines diverse aspects of aging. Geriatrics, on the other hand, focuses on:
- a. early childhood development
- b. maturation
- X c. clinical aspects of aging
- d. economic well-being in old age

(M) 8. Changes in the organism throughout the life span occur in sequence. This sequence consists of the following steps:
- a. development and maturation
- X b. development, maturation, senescence
- c. birth and maturation
- d. aging and development

(E) 9. Demands that the social and physical environment place on the individual are known as:
- a. environmental congruence
- X b. environmental press
- c. transactions
- d. dynamic interactions

(E) 10. The theoretical upper limit of an individual's ability to function in health, cognition and behavior is known as:
- X a. individual competence
- b. social press
- c. individual adaptability
- d. maturation

(M) 11. It is difficult to generalize about the older population because:

- a. aging can be defined only in multiple domains
- b. the older population is tremendously diverse
- c. there can be a range of 30 years between the young-old and the oldest-old
- X d. all of the above
- e. none of the above

(M) 12. As societies become more advanced with improvements in health care and sanitation, the survival curve becomes:
- a. flatter
- X b. more rectangular
- c. steeper
- d. bimodal

4

(M) 13. Population pyramids for the US will become:

X   a.   more rectangular
      b.   more pyramid-like
      c.   difficult to project
      d.   elongated

(E) 14. The state with the highest proportion of older people in its population today is _____; that with the lowest is _____.

X   a.   Florida/Alaska
      b.   Florida/Utah
      c.   Arkansas/South Dakota
      d.   Iowa/Rhode Island

(M) 15. Compared to the United States, the ratio of workers to retirees in Japan and Europe is becoming _____.
      a.   more pyramid-like
      b.   less rectangular
      c.   greater
X   d.   smaller

(M) 16. The growing discrepancy between the poor and non-poor in the US is expected to lead to:
      a.   class wars
      b.   more need for hospitals for older persons
X   c.   a bimodal distribution of healthy and frail elders
      d.   more women remaining healthy, more men dying younger

(M) 17. The distinction between active and dependent life expectancy is useful in illustrating:

      a.   differences between men and women
X   b.   that not all gains in life expectancy are positive
      c.   that most of the gain in life expectancy is a negative gain
      d.   the advantages of increased life expectancy for ethnic minorities

(E) 18. The earliest research centers (pre-1960) established to study gerontology include all except the following:
      a.   The Baltimore City Hospital
X   b.   The National Institute on Aging
      c.   The Duke University Center on Aging
      d.   The University of Chicago Center on Aging

(M) 19. A major advantage of longitudinal research designs is that they:

          a.   allow for practice effects
X   b.   eliminate cohort effects
          c.   allow a distinction between age and time by testing
          d.   compare different groups

(M) 20. A research design that alleviates the problems of cross-sectional and longitudinal studies, and is useful for distinguishing between age and historical factors, is known as a:
          a.   sequential design
X   b.   time-sequential design
          c.   cohort-sequential design
          d.   cross-sequential design

(C) 21. A researcher wants to examine changing attitudes toward welfare among people of different cohorts. She conducts interviews with people born in 1930 and 1950 during 1985, and again in 1995. This is an example of a:
          a.   longitudinal design
          b.   cohort-sequential design
X   c.   cross-sequential design
          d.   time-sequential design

(M) 22. Testing people's fear of flying shortly following a major airplane crash might produce a(n):
          a.   age effect
X   b.   time-of-measurement effect
          c.   practice effect
          d.   cohort effect

(M) 23. Which two effects are confounded in cross-sectional research?

X   a.   age and cohort
          b.   age and time-of-measurement
          c.   cohort and time-of-measurement
          d.   cohort and practice

(M) 24. Which two effects are confounded in longitudinal research?

          a.   age and cohort
X   b.   age and time-of-measurement
          c.   cohort and time-of-measurement
          d.   cohort and practice

(M) 25. A valid measure is one that:

        a.   yields the same result from repeated measurements

X   b.   accurately reflects the concept it is intended to measure

        c.   is used only in cross-sectional studies

        d.   is used only in psychological testing

(C) 26. A researcher wants to determine the range of oral disease among the older population by examining the mouths of all 200 residents of a nursing home. The findings cannot be generalized to all older people because:

        a.   the sample is not valid

        b.   the data are not reliable

        c.   the concept is not correctly measured

X   d.   the sample is not representative

(C) 27. The problem of trying to reach ethnic minority elders from the membership list of AARP is that:

X   a.   they are under-represented in this group

        b.   only the sickest are likely to be members

        c.   they are over-represented in this group

        d.   they do not represent the geographic diversity of ethnic groups

(M) 28. Selective dropout from longitudinal studies results in:

        a.   poorer test scores with time

X   b.   healthier and more motivated elders in the final sample

        c.   sicker and less educated elders in the final sample

        d.   few differences between drop-outs and those who remain

True or False

(E) 1. In general, the chronological age of most people is consistent with their psychological and biological age.

       True ___   False <u>X</u>

(E) 2. The cohort of young-old people today has lived through the Great Depression.

       True <u>X</u>   False ___

(M) 3. Relocation to an unfamiliar environment is an example of increased environmental press in Lawton and Nahemow's model.

       True <u>X</u>   False ___

(M) 4. Older people who are experiencing declines in competence would benefit from a move to a nursing home.

       True ___   False <u>X</u>

(E) 5. The study of aging is primarily a study of diseases.

       True ___   False <u>X</u>

(M) 6. Life expectancy refers to the average years of life one can expect to live, whereas maximum life span refers to the maximum number of years a given species is expected to live.

       True <u>X</u>   False ___

(M) 7. In 1985 the US had proportionately more people over age 65 in its population than did any other industrial country.

       True ___   False <u>X</u>

(M) 8. Today, life expectancy among older minorities is very similar to that of whites.

       True ___   False <u>X</u>

(M) 9. The proportion of people aged 65 and older among ethnic minority groups will remain essentially unchanged in the 21st century.

       True ___   False <u>X</u>

(M) 10. Surveys of the health status of young-old Americans today provide considerable support for compressed morbidity in the future.

       True <u>X</u>   False ___

(E) 11. The greatest proportion of elders in the US live in central cities.

       True ___   False <u>X</u>

(E) 12. Cross-sectional research designs are the best method to determine causation.

       True ___   False <u>X</u>

(M) 13. Older people who drop out of longitudinal studies tend to be those who score lower on intelligence tests and are more socially isolated.

        True <u>X</u>   False ___

(E) 14. Longitudinal studies are currently the most widely used research designs in gerontology.

        True ___   False <u>X</u>

(M) 15. Sequential designs are particularly useful in studies of cognitive changes with aging.

        True <u>X</u>   False ___

CHAPTER 2: HISTORICAL AND CROSS-CULTURAL ISSUES IN AGING

Glossary

Comparative sociocultural gerontology
Geronticide
Senecide
Modernization
Social stratification
Veneration of elders
Filial piety

Sources of power:
 *property
 *political
 *knowledge
Reciprocity
Acceptance of dependency
Traditional/transitional societies

Topics for Discussion

1. What has been the impact of modernization on the status and role of older people in different cultures?

2. What specific aspects of modernization contribute to a change in older people's social status? In addition to modernization, what other reasons explain changes between generations in American society?

3. What factors may influence the differential social status of older people in different societies at the same stage of modernization?

4. To what extent can older people maintain power in a social system through control of knowledge and property? Describe any gender differences that may arise in this ability to control resources.

5. It has been suggested that the study of aging in other cultures is of intrinsic interest but has no relevance to an understanding of old age in our own society. Argue the pros and cons of this proposition.

6. Discuss the changing status and roles of older people from prehistoric through colonial times.

7. What influence does the physical and cognitive status of an older person have on society's response toward older people in general?

8. Discuss the role of economic changes in societies such as Japan and China on filial piety and on the status of multigenerational households.

Broke down into 5 groups.
Each group examined and answered one of the above questions marked with a ✿.

10

Multiple Choice

(M) 1. Old age in prehistoric times was characterized by all of the following factors <u>except</u>:

        a.   respect and a sense of sacred obligation toward elders
        b.   geronticide toward the very old and unhealthy
X   c.   multiple children available to care for elders
        d.   geronticide being carried out with great reverence

(M) 2. In classical civilizations, the aged who benefited the most from respect to elders were:

        a.   all men
        b.   all older people
X   c.   men from the elite classes
        d.   mothers of the tribal leaders

(M) 3. The growth of democracy in fifth century Greece was generally associated with:

        a.   increasing veneration of the aged
X   b.   increasing exaltation of youth
        c.   respect for older people's power
        d.   respect for wisdom

(M) 4. Old age in Colonial America was characterized by:

X   a.   veneration toward elders
        b.   considerable affection or love for elders
        c.   low status of elders
        d.   frequent interaction between young and old

(M) 5. In the 19th and 20th centuries, demographic patterns shifted so that:

X   a.   parents generally lived many more years after their children left home
        b.   more older people assumed positions of prestige and power
        c.   more older people were dependent on their children
        d.   more multigenerational families lived together

(C) 6. According to modernization theory, the status of the older population has declined for all the following reasons <u>except</u>:
        a.   health technology that has prolonged adult life
X   b.   more older people remaining in the work force
        c.   efforts to promote literacy and education
        d.   urbanization

(M) 7. Among the important resources controlled by older people that enhance their positions in society, which is the least important one?
   a.   knowledge of traditional skills
X b.   chronological age
   c.   information control
   d.   their social contributions

(M) 8. According to Fischer, the decline in older people's status is due to:

   a.   industrialization and civilization
   b.   the increase in the number of older people
X c.   our cultural values of liberty and equality
   d.   modernization

(M) 9. The major premise of modernization theory is that with modernization:

   a.   the status of older people always increases
   b.   there are more opportunities for intergenerational interaction
   c.   older people experience a higher quality of life
X d.   older people often lose political and social power

(M) 10. A popular alternative to modernization theory suggests that the shift toward a capitalist economy aided the development of:

X a.   retirement laws
   b.   adult children caring for elders
   c.   work opportunities after retirement
   d.   early entry into the workforce

(M) 11. As wealth became an increasing source of social identity in America, there was a shift in the 19th and 20th centuries toward:

   a.   greater prestige accorded the older population
   b.   declining intergenerational ties
   c.   growing recognition of the need to support older family members
X d.   growing veneration of youth and contempt of old age

(M) 12. Which of the following statements about the care of older persons in Japan is true?

    a.   Traditionally, Japanese families have cared for their members, and this pattern has not changed significantly.

    b.   Japanese families assume no more responsibility for their older relatives than do Western families.

X   c.   Traditionally, Japanese families have cared for their older relatives, but that pattern is eroding.

    d.   The old are such a small proportion of the Japanese population that their care is not a significant problem.

(M) 13. Knowledge as a source of power for older people is often undermined in societies where:

X   a.   scientific advances supersede traditional knowledge

    b.   money assumes decreased value

    c.   rituals become less formal

    d.   educational institutions reject the contributions of older members

(M) 14. The traditional roles of older adults in Japan have changed as a result of all except the following:

    a.   increased urbanization

    b.   declining birthrate

    c.   more women in the labor force

X   d.   Western influence regarding age equity

(M) 15. Which of the following is not a traditional source of power for older people in most societies?

    a.   control of property

X   b.   government benefits that accrue to older members

    c.   filial piety within the extended family

    d.   knowledge

(M) 16. Benign neglect of older people is generally accepted:

    a.   in all modern societies

    b.   in traditional societies

X   c.   in some societies when the elder is physically or cognitively impaired

    d.   in some societies when the elder provides no financial help to the family

(E) 17. One way in which older adults maintain a feeling of being connected with other generations over time is through:

    a.   separation

    b.   acculturation

X   c.   rituals

    d.   continuity

(E) 18.   The key aspect for old men at the top is control of:

        a.   animals
        b.   children
X   c.   power
        d.   women

(M)19.   In response to changes in multigenerational living arrangements in Japan, the national government of Japan:

X   a.   offers a tax credit to people providing elder care
        b.   provides free nursing home care for frail elders
        c.   penalizes families who do not help their aging parents
        d.   encourages people to build cottages for their retirement

True or False

(E) 1. Comparative sociocultural gerontology allows us to study the biological processes of aging.

       True ___   False X

(M) 2. Old age was first defined in chronological terms (e.g., age 60 and over) in Greek and Roman cultures.

       True X   False ___

(M) 3. The increase in median age that occurred in the early 19th century was due primarily to the declining death rate.

       True ___   False X

(M) 4. In most societies, older people's status is largely determined by the balance between their perceived contributions to society and the cost of maintaining them.

       True X   False ___

(E) 5. Shakespeare's view of old age is that of wisdom and social perspective.

       True ___   False X

(E) 6. Old age was viewed as a sign of God's favor by the Puritans.

       True X   False ___

(M) 7. The Colonial era is marked by a time of close intergenerational bonds.

       True ___   False X

(M) 8. Filial piety was generally reserved for older people of higher social classes in traditional Chinese culture.

       True X   False ___

(M) 9. In nineteenth century America, egalitarian values did not extend to economic equality; old age no longer was equated with economic power.

       True X   False ___

(M) 10. Filial piety in traditional cultures can be significantly undermined in societies if resources become scarce.

       True X   False ___

(M) 11. Older people have been able to retain their positions of prestige in most societies by continuing to be employed.

       True ___   False X

(E) 12. In some religious groups, the most sacred rituals are reserved for the elders of that group.

        True X   False ___

(E) 13. Some social historians have criticized modernization theory for idealizing family structures in pre-industrial societies.

        True X   False ___

(M) 14. Despite its advanced industrial status, Japan has maintained strong intergenerational relations by continuing the pattern of retired elders moving in with the oldest son and his family.

        True ___   False X

(M) 15. Societies that encourage home care of frail elders generally rely on paid caregivers, not family members.

        True ___   False X

CHAPTER 3: THE SOCIAL CONSEQUENCES OF PHYSIOLOGICAL AGING

Glossary

Accommodation
Aerobic Capacity
Atherosclerosis
Atrophic Gastritis
Auditory Canal
Autoimmune Theory of Aging
Cataracts
Cellular Aging Theory of Aging
Cilia
Cross Linkage Theory of Aging
Dementia
Diastolic Blood Pressure
Electroencephalogram
Epidermis
Esophagus
Estrogen
Free Radical Theory of Aging
Functional Capacity
Glaucoma
Glial Cells
Glucose
Hyperthermia
Hyponatremia
Hypothermia
Inner Ear
Kinesthetic System
Kyphosis
Macular Degeneration
Melanin
Menopause

Middle Ear
Morbidity
Neurons
Neurotransmitters
Nocturnal Myoclonus
Orthopedic Injuries
Osteoporosis
Perception
Pinna
Presbycusis
Recognition Threshold
REM
Renal Function
Senescence
Sensation
Sensory Discrimination
Sensory Threshold
Sleep Apnea
Sleep Hygiene
Synapse
Systolic Blood Pressure
Testosterone
Tinnitus
Triglycerides
Tympanic Membrane
Urinary Incontinence
Varicosities
Vertigo

Topics for Discussion

1.   Several biological theories of aging have emerged over the past 20 years. Provide a critical analysis of each theory in terms of how it helps our understanding of the aging process, and its potential for reversing that process.

2.   Discuss some of the recent discoveries with human growth hormones and their effects of extending the life span and/or active life expectancy.

3.   In what ways could specific changes in body composition with aging influence an older person's reactions to medications and alcohol?

4.   Discuss some physiological and environmental risk factors for hypothermia in older people. What environmental interventions could be provided to alleviate these risks?

5.   Discuss the problem of hyperthermia in older people. What are the individual and environmental risk factors involved? How can hypothermia affect the older person's cognitive functions?

6.   Describe how people adapt to declines in several areas of physiological functioning with age.

7.   Compare normal, age-related changes in different organ systems. Which systems show the greatest change? Which the least? Suggest environmental interventions to alleviate the impact of some of these organ system changes on the older person.

8.   Provide three examples of normal, age-related changes in visual functioning and three examples of pathological aging. To what extent can environmental interventions aid the older person undergoing these changes?

9.   There are numerous structural changes in the eye and the ear with aging that may influence older people's visual and auditory functioning. Describe these structural changes, and explain to what extent these changes versus changes in central processes may affect visual and auditory functioning.

10.   In what ways does hearing loss affect the older person's environmental competence?

11.   Describe some communication techniques and environmental interventions that may be used by professionals working with older people who have hearing and vision impairments.

12.   There is some debate about the role of structural changes versus social behavior in older people's complaints about their taste and olfactory acuity. Present evidence for each set of factors regarding their impact on older people's enjoyment of food and fragrances.

13.   Discuss the importance of using more refined measurement techniques to assess age-related changes in taste and olfaction.

14.   To what extent are complaints of pain an indication of changes in tactile sensitivity vs. personality and social expectations among older persons?

15.   Discuss the impact of multiple sensory impairments occurring simultaneously on the need to modify an older person's physical environment.

Multiple Choice

(E) 1. Organ systems decline at differing rates among people. All of the following factors influence senescence <u>except</u>:

X   a.   level of education
      b.   heredity
      c.   physical activity
      d.   environmental toxins and stress

(M) 2. The biological theory that proposes that each species has a biological clock that determines its maximum life span and the rate at which each organ system will deteriorate is known as:

      a.   disengagement
      b.   the cross-linkage theory
X   c.   the wear and tear theory
      d.   the antioxidant theory

(M) 3. According to the free radical theory, the aging process may be slowed down with the ingestion of:

X   a.   ~~Beta Carotene~~ Antioxidants
      b.   Vitamin C
      c.   Vitamin D
      d.   Lecithin

(M) 4. All of the following interventions have been shown to improve active life expectancy in lab animals <u>except</u>:

      a.   vitamin E
      b.   growth hormones
X   c.   increased sleep
      d.   caloric restriction

(M) 5. All of the following changes occur in body composition with advancing age except an increase in:

      a.   the proportion of fat
      b.   fibrous material
      c.   the sodium/potassium ratio
X   d.   the proportion of water

(M) 6. Changes in the temperature regulatory system with aging result in a preference by older persons for ambient temperatures that are:

      a.   much warmer than for younger people
      b.   much cooler than for younger people
      c.   a few degrees cooler than for younger people
X   d.   a few degrees warmer than for younger people

(M) 7. With aging, vital capacity:

        a.   declines at a similar rate among all people
X   b.   declines more rapidly among sedentary people
        c.   is impaired primarily because of environmental pollutants
        d.   is equally impaired in smokers and non-smokers

(M) 8. Physical training among sedentary older persons has been shown to result in:

        a.   increased death rates
        b.   significant reductions in cholesterol levels
        c.   reduced vital capacity
X   d.   significant increases in aerobic capacity

(M) 9. Among all organ systems, the one that has been found to decline most in structure and function with normal aging is:
        a.   the respiratory system
        b.   the heart
X   c.   the kidneys
        d.   the central nervous system

(M) 10. Studies of "master athletes" and other people who maintain a rigorous physical exercise regimen have concluded that aging occurs later in which function below?
X   a.   stamina
        b.   strength
        c.   neuromuscular coordination
        d.   vital capacity

(E) 11. Urinary incontinence among older people generally is <u>not</u> due to:

        a.   a decline in the capacity of the bladder
        b.   diseases associated with the nervous system
        c.   changes in the brain that affect the sensation to void
X   d.   increased consumption of tea and coffee

(M) 12. Slower reaction time with aging is most likely due to:

X   a.   slower response of neurotransmitters
        b.   a rapid accumulation of lipofuscin in the brain
        c.   a loss of brain mass
        d.   anxiety about test taking

(M)13. Older people often have more problems seeing under low lighting conditions. This is least likely due to:
    a.   a reduction in the maximum opening of the pupil
    b.   a slower shift from rods to cones
    c.   a reduced supply of oxygen to the retina
X   d.   glaucoma

(M) 14. Collagen tissue changes the composition and elasticity of the lens with aging. This results in problems with:
    a.   visual acuity
    b.   peripheral vision
X   c.   accommodation
    d.   depth perception

(M) 15. A common cause of vision loss among older persons that increases almost linearly with age, and may be related to a deficiency in antioxidants is:
X   a.   cataracts
    b.   senile macular degeneration
    c.   diabetic retinopathy
    d.   glaucoma

(C) 16. Glaucoma results in increased problems with _____, whereas macular degeneration impairs _____.
X   a.   peripheral vision/central vision
    b.   central vision/peripheral vision
    c.   accommodation/acuity
    d.   color perception/discrimination

(M) 17. The best strategy for an older person who is experiencing age-related problems with vision is to:
    a.   see a psychiatrist
    b.   stop participating in activities outside the house
X   c.   modify the home environment to make it congruent with changing needs
    d.   turn to friends and relatives who can take over some responsibilities at home

(E) 18. With aging, there is increased difficulty in distinguishing between the following colors:

X   a.   blue and green
    b.   green and orange
    c.   red and yellow
    d.   red and orange

(M) 19. The structural change with aging that is most associated with hearing loss takes place in:
- a. the pinna
- X   b. the cochlea
- c. the stapes
- d. the middle ear

(M) 20. A major reason why many older people avoid using hearing aids is:

- X   a. they raise the volume of background noises
- b. they make it difficult to hear oneself talk
- c. they are a problem to keep clean
- d. they are unattractive

(M) 21. Olfactory sensitivity in aging:

- a. deteriorates significantly
- b. shows greater decline than taste acuity
- X   c. is retained among women more than men
- d. declines because of a significant reduction in the number of olfactory receptors

(M) 22. Increased complaints of physical pain among older people are:

- X   a. often a sign of depression
- b. due to a lower threshold for pain with aging
- c. due to a higher threshold for pain with aging
- d. a normal concomitant of aging

(M) 23. The kinesthetic system appears to change with aging, such that older people:

- a. become confused with visual cues
- X   b. need more visual and surface cues
- c. prefer walking faster
- d. have difficulty with their tactile sensitivity

(E) 24. An older person who is experiencing problems with depth perception could improve their home environment by:
- X   a. using color contrast where different levels meet
- b. using bright patterns on carpets throughout the house
- c. avoiding dark colors
- d. putting signs at the top of every stairway

(M) 25. Researchers examining several different hormones in animal studies have found that:

      a.   growth hormones injected in old rats make them taller

X   b.   growth hormones injected in old female rats improve protein synthesis

      c.   the loss of hormones affects physical stamina among old rats

      d.   the loss of estrogen in female rats makes them aggressive

True or False

(E) 1. Aging may be attributable to the finite number of cell replications as the organism ages chronologically, according to one biological theory of aging.
      True X   False ___

(E) 2. Theories of biological aging now provide scientists with adequate knowledge to begin experiments to reverse the aging process.
      True ___   False X

(E) 3. Wound healing takes place more slowly in older people.
      True X   False ___

(E) 4. Osteoporosis is a normal change in the musculoskeletal system with aging.
      True ___   False X

(E) 5. Normal aging is accompanied by a slight increase in systolic blood pressure.
      True X   False ___

(M) 6. Changes in the size and function of the liver with aging result in greater sensitivity to medications that are metabolized by the liver.
      True X   False ___

(M) 7. Older people should reduce their intake of caffeine and alcohol because these substances inhibit the production of ADH.
      True X   False ___

(M) 8. Neuronal loss with aging is the primary reason for older people's forgetfulness.
      True ___   False X

(M) 9. Generally, older adults report that they sleep longer and deeper than when they were younger.
      True ___   False X

(M) 10. Changes in circadian rhythms with aging appear to be associated with changes in core body temperatures.
      True X   False ___

(M) 11. The best replacement lens for an older person who has had a cataract is a contact lens.
      True ___   False X

(M) 12. Increased problems with glare are generally attributable to uneven hardening of the lens.
      True X   False ___

(M) 13. Glaucoma is both more prevalent and more difficult to treat in African Americans.
True _X_   False ___

(M) 14. Tinnitus is a common condition among older people that can result in permanent deafness.
True ___   False _X_

(M) 15. Contrary to earlier studies of taste and aging, recent researchers have found little evidence of taste bud loss with aging.
True _X_   False ___

(M) 16. Recent studies of taste acuity among older people have shown only minimal changes in taste thresholds for most of the primary tastes.
True _X_   False ___

(M) 17. The kinesthetic system is one of the few sensory functions that remain intact with aging.
True ___   False _X_

(M) 18. Researchers have found that aging results in a higher pain tolerance.
True _X_   False ___

CHAPTER 4: MANAGING CHRONIC DISEASES, AND PROMOTING WELL-BEING IN OLD AGE

Glossary

ADL
Acute vs. Chronic Condition
Arteriosclerosis
Benign Hypertrophy of the Prostate
Contracture
Diverticulitis
Disability
DRG
Edentulous
Good Health
Health Promotion

Health Status
Hiatus Hernia
Hypokinesia
Iatrogenic Disease
Immunity
Incontinence
Osteopenia
Rheumatoid Arthritis
Stress

Topics for Discussion

1. What are some of the implications of current research findings for the relationship between particular risk factors and illness?

2. If you were developing a health promotion program to encourage older people to visit physicians for preventive purposes, what approach would you utilize? Briefly describe the major components of your health promotion program.

3. Discuss how socio-cultural factors (demographics, cultural values) influence:
   a. evaluations of health
   b. health status
   c. health behavior
   d. utilization of health care services

4. Describe the major causes of AIDS in older men and women. How would you design an education program on AIDS for this population vs. a younger audience?

Multiple Choice

(E) 1.   Compared to women aged 70 to 74, those who are 90 and older are about _____ times more likely to need some assistance in their activities of daily living.

        a.   2
X   b.   3
        c.   5
        d.   8

(E) 2.   Most older people perceive their own health as being_____ the health of their peers.

X   a.   better than
        b.   about the same
        c.   worse than
        d.   much worse than

(E) 3.   Vaccinations against influenza and pneumonia:

        a.   are more effective for children than for older people
        b.   are routinely obtained by most older people
X   c.   can improve morbidity and mortality rates of elders
        d.   have recently been excluded from Medicare reimbursements

(M) 4.   Which of the following statements is true?

        a.   The incidence of acute and chronic disease increases with age.
        b.   The incidence of acute diseases increases with age.
X   c.   Older men have fewer chronic conditions than older women.
        d.   Biological factors play almost no role in gender differences related to health.
        e.   none of the above

(E) 5.   The most common chronic condition among persons age 65 and over is:

        a.   arteriosclerosis
        b.   hypertension
        c.   hearing impairments
X   d.   arthritis

(M) 6.   Which of the following is not true of chronic health conditions?

        a.   Most older people have at least one.
X   b.   They are short-term.
        c.   The cause is unknown for most.
        d.   Cures are currently not available.

(M) 7. Older African Americans have a disproportionately higher incidence of:

        a.   arteriosclerosis
X   b.   hypertension
        c.   cerebrovascular disease
        d.   osteoporosis

(E) 8. The major cause of death among people age 65 and older is:

X   a.   heart disease
        b.   cancer
        c.   stroke
        d.   accidents and suicide

(E) 9. The major risk factor for cardiovascular disease is:

        a.   hypotension
X   b.   hypertension
        c.   atherosclerosis
        d.   diabetes

(E) 10. Osteoporosis is a major risk factor for:

        a.   significant weight loss in older people
        b.   problems with bladder control
X   c.   hip fractures
        d.   strokes

(E) 11. Osteoporosis occurs among:

        a.   women only
        b.   people over age 80 only
        c.   men only
X   d.   mostly women after the menopause

(M) 12. Risk factors for hip fractures include all of the following except:

        a.   age over 70
X   b.   long-term estrogen use
        c.   being a white female
        d.   use of medications that affect balance

(M) 13. Currently the recommended methods of preventing osteoporosis include all except:

X   a.   fluoride tablets
        b.   hormone replacement therapy begun during menopause
        c.   synthetic calcitonin
        d.   increased intake of calcium and Vitamin D

(M)14. Older people with incontinence:

        a.   cannot be treated
X   b.   should be examined for reversible causes
        c.   can generally be treated with medications only
        d.   consume more fluids

(E) 15. The primary cause of AIDS in people over age 70 today is:
X   a.   blood transfusions
        b.   homosexual contact
        c.   heterosexual contact
        d.   IV drug use

(M) 16. Compared to young adults, older persons:
        a.   are less likely to be victims of pedestrian accidents
        b.   are less likely to die from injuries sustained in an accident
X   c.   have more auto accidents per mile driven
        d.   have more accidents due to drunken driving

(M) 17. The risk of death due to trauma (i.e. physical injuries in 80 year olds is _____ the rate in 20 year olds.
        a.   1/2
        b.   2 times
X   c.   4 times
        d.   10 times

(M) 18. Risk factors for falls include all of the following except:
        a.   inactivity
        b.   visual impairments
        c.   medications that can cause postural hypotension
X   d.   overexertion

(M) 19. National surveys of physician use in the United States reveal that people over age 65 are _____ more likely to visit a physician within one year than people in younger age groups:

    a.   twice

    b.   three times

X   c.   slightly

    d.   significantly

(M) 20. All of the following are limitations of health promotion programs with older adult except:

    a.   most health promotion efforts have been short-term demonstration projects

    b.   most health promotion programs have focused on the well population

    c.   funding for continuing such programs is limited

X   d.   most programs encourage seeking more medical services than necessary

True or False

(M) 1. Older people are likely to spend more days of restricted activity due to acute conditions than middle-aged people because they experience more incidents of acute disease.

        True ___   False _X_

(E) 2. A factor that appears to be significantly related to life satisfaction is perceptions of one's health.

        True _X_   False ___

(E) 3. Significant increases in blood pressure are a universal corollary of aging.

        True ___   False _X_

(E) 4. Cerebrovascular accident (CVA) refers to a type of heart attack.

        True ___   False _X_

(E) 5. The most important treatment for arthritis is to limit any physical activity.

        True ___   False _X_

(M) 6. The symptoms of diabetes are difficult to detect in older people.

        True _X_   False ___

(M) 7. The most common form of diabetes in older people is one that develops late and requires daily use of insulin.

        True ___   False _X_

(E) 8. Stress incontinence is best treated with medications.

        True ___   False _X_

(E) 9. Constipation is a normal part of the aging process.

        True ___   False _X_

(E) 10. Older people may be more vulnerable to AIDS than younger persons because the immune system deteriorates with aging.

        True _X_   False ___

(M) 11. Because older people are aware of their risk of contracting AIDS, they are more likely to use condoms than younger adults.

        True ___   False _X_

(E) 12. There is little that we can do in our personal health practices to alter our active life expectancy.

        True ___   False _X_

(E) 13. Health promotion programs should attempt to improve the general environment as well as individual health practices.

        True <u>X</u>   False ___

(E) 14. Health promotion does not improve the physical functioning of people aged 75+.

        True ___   False <u>X</u>

(M) 15. Older people who are injured in auto accidents have a greater risk of hospitalization and death than do young persons.

        True <u>X</u>   False ___

CHAPTER 5: COGNITIVE CHANGES WITH AGING

Glossary

General factor theory
Structure of intelligence
Intelligence quotient (IQ)
Fluid intelligence
Crystallized intelligence
Wechsler Adult Intelligence Scale (WAIS)
Classic Aging Pattern
Primary mental abilities
Terminal drop hypothesis
Selective attrition
Errors of omission
Errors of commission
Divergent thinking

Learning
Memory
Sensory memory
*Iconic memory
*Echoic memory
Primary memory
Secondary memory
Spatial memory
Information processing model
Mnemonics
Method of Loci
Creativity

Topics for Discussion

1. Discuss examples of changes in crystallized and fluid intelligence with aging. In what ways could methodological problems result in exaggerating declines in these two types of intelligence?

2. Discuss the advantages and disadvantages of longitudinal research designs to study intelligence in old age.

3. To what extent do changes in sensory processes and physiological functioning affect older people's memory at the stages of sensory, primary and secondary memory?

4. In what ways can the learning environment be enhanced to improve learning ability and retention of newly acquired information in the older learner? What factors can disrupt older people's acquisition of new information?

5. Studies of learning among younger people have found an inverse U-function between anxiety and performance, such that a moderate level of anxiety is associated with optimal learning. To what extent does this model apply to older learners?

6. In what ways have older persons been found to compensate for declines in information processing and perceptual-motor speed?

Multiple Choice

(M) 1. All of the following represent dimensions in Guilford's model of intellect <u>except</u>:

        a.   operations
        b.   contents
X   c.   performance
        d.   products

(E) 2. The component of intelligence that consists of skills acquired through a lifetime of experiences and education is known as:

        a.   fluid intelligence
X   b.   crystallized intelligence
        c.   primary mental abilities
        d.   omnibus intelligence

(M) 3. The Classic Aging Pattern is the term used to describe:

        a.   decline on all subtests of the WAIS after age 50
        b.   decline on verbal scales of the WAIS after age 60
X   c.   decline on performance scales of the WAIS after age 65
        d.   improvement on the WAIS between 55 and 75; significant drops after 75

(M) 4. A 75-year-old retired English teacher who still volunteers as a tutor is tested on the verbal scales of the WAIS. Compared to her scores on these same scales at age 45, the Classic Aging Pattern would predict:

        a.   significantly worse performance at age 75
        b.   significantly better performance at age 75
        c.   improvement on some scales, decline on others
X   d.   generally the same scores at both times

(M) 5. Selective attrition from longitudinal studies of intellectual functioning often results in the inaccurate conclusion that:

X   a.   intellectual functioning remains stable or improves over time.
        b.   intellectual functioning declines significantly over time.
        c.   older people who volunteer for studies of intelligence are the least healthy.
        d.   older people who survive in these studies are slower than others.

(M) 6. A major longitudinal study of intelligence in older persons that has resulted in the development of sequential research designs is the:

    a.   New York State Study of Twins
    b.   Iowa State Study
X   c.   Seattle Longitudinal Study
    d.   Duke Longitudinal Studies

(M) 7. Adult intelligence appears to be influenced by all of the following variables except:

    a.   education
    b.   physical health
    c.   employment in complex vs. simple jobs
X   d.   psychomotor speed

(C) 8. Performance on tests of intelligence by older persons with borderline hypertension, compared to those with normal blood pressure, has been found to be:

    a.   worse
X   b.   better
    c.   about the same
    d.   has not been tested

(E) 9. The decline in intelligence test scores just before death is known as:

    a.   selective attrition
    b.   psychomotor slowing
X   c.   terminal drop
    d.   retrieval abilities

(E) 10. The process of encoding new information into one's memory is known as:

X   a.   learning
    b.   intelligence
    c.   iconic memory
    d.   sensory memory

(M) 11. New information first enters the pre-attentive stage for a few milliseconds. This is known as:
    a.   primary memory
    b.   spatial memory
    c.   iconic memory
X   d.   sensory memory

(C) 12. Schaie's work shows changes in primary mental abilities (PMAs) over 7 years in older people. Which of the following statements is not true?

        a.   all ages > 60 retain at least one PMA

X   b.   by age 81, only 10% of people retain 4 or more PMAs.

        c.   By age 81, almost 50% retain 4 or more PMAs

        d.   by age 60, 40% retain all PMAs

(M) 13. Recent studies have shown that older people's performance on tests of intelligence is influenced by all of the following factors except:

        a.   nutritional deficiencies

        b.   depression

        c.   dysphoria

X   d.   cohort

(E) 14. Studies of primary memory in older people have found:

        a.   they can recall less than 4 pieces of information

X   b.   they can recall 7 ± 2 pieces of information

        c.   significantly poorer recall than among younger persons

        d.   much better short-term recall than long-term recall

(C) 15. You are designing an aptitude test to hire older people as computer programmers. The best way to assess their skills would be:

        a.   give them several opportunities to guess the answer

        b.   use a timed test

X   c.   use a self-paced test

        d.   tell them the stakes are high

(M) 16. Which of the following factors is least likely to affect the efficiency of primary memory in older people?

X   a.   storage capacity of the older brain

        b.   slower reaction time

        c.   decline in attentional resources

        d.   problems with divided attention

(E) 17. Age related deficiencies have been found in tests of_____, but not in tests of
_____.

        a.   recognition/recall

X   b.   recall/recognition

        c.   primary memory/secondary memory

        d.   distant events/recent events

(M) 18. Studies of typing skill in typists ranging from age 19 to 72 have revealed all the following changes with age <u>except</u> that older typists:

    a.   have slower reaction time than young typists
    b.   can complete the task in the same time as young typists
X   c.   cannot compensate for slower perceptual-motor speed
    d.   make more efficient moves on the task

(M) 19. Associating new information with an image has been found to be useful for older people as a:
    a.   method of finding their way around a new place
    b.   method of enhancing creativity
    c.   way of remembering where they have placed their belongings
X   d.   method of visualizing newly learned words or concepts

(C) 20. Researchers who have tested the pros and cons of cognitive retraining programs have found that:
X   a.   older people benefit less than younger people
    b.   they are effective when combined with memory-enhancing drugs
    c.   booster sessions make them ideal for older people
    d.   verbal mediators are better than visual methods for older people

(M) 21. List-making is most helpful for older people who:

X   a.   have strong vocabulary skills
    b.   have the least education
    c.   have Alzheimer's disease
    d.   take a lot of medications

(M) 22. Studies of wisdom in older adults:

    a.   reveal increased levels as the person ages
    b.   reveal declining levels as the person ages
X   c.   show high life satisfaction in people who have achieved wisdom
    d.   have generally used tests of convergent thinking

(M) 23. Studies of creativity:

    a.   show that creative young children become creative elders
    b.   have examined problem solving skills of artists and scientists
X   c.   generally have examined the creative output of artists and scientists
    d.   generally rely on self-reports of creativity

True or False

(E) 1. It is generally agreed by researchers that most types of intelligence decline after age 60.
        True ____   False_X

(E) 2. Studies of health status and performance on tests of intelligence reveal greater decline among those with uncontrolled blood pressure.
        True _X   False ____

(M) 3. Researchers have found inconsistent results regarding the ability to use abstract thought processes in old age.
        True _X   False ____

(M) 4. Declines in intelligence test scores by older people have been found to be due primarily to lower psychomotor functioning.
        True ____   False_X

(M) 5. The Seattle Longitudinal Study has demonstrated that, by age 80, there is a significant decline for most people in at least 3 primary mental abilities.
        True ____   False_X

(M) 6. Older subjects make more errors of omission than errors of commission in tests of paired associates.
        True _X   False ____

(M) 7. Long-term memory appears to deteriorate with aging because of information overload.
        True ____   False_X

(E) 8. Older persons perform better than younger subjects when given the chance to give creative responses under conditions of uncertainty and high risk.
        True ____   False_X

(E) 9. Older subjects perform much worse than younger persons on tests of free recall.
        True _X   False ____

(M) 10. Older people have more problems with spatial memory than do younger people, unless multiple visual cues are used.
        True _X   False ____

(C) 11. Creativity appears to change in an inverted U-pattern with age, peaking at age 30 and declining steadily to age 70.
        True ___   False_X

(C) 12. Most older people are more likely than younger persons to have achieved wisdom because they have been able to reflect on their worldly experiences.
        True ___   False_X

CHAPTER 6: PERSONALITY AND MENTAL HEALTH

Glossary

Active and Passive Mastery
Adaptation
Anxiety Disorder
Archetypes
Benign Senescent Disorder
Coping
  *Emotion Focused
  *Problem Focused
Defense mechanisms
Dementia
Depression (major vs. minor or reactive)
Ego Integrity vs. Despair
Electroconvulsive or Electroshock Therapy (ECT)
Generativity

Life Events
Life Structures
Paranoia
Psychopathology
Self-concept
Self-esteem
Stage Theories of Personality
Successful Aging
Reminiscence Therapy
Trait Theories

Topics for Discussion

1.   Discuss some differences between stage and trait theories of personality. Give some examples of each type.

2.   Self-concept is generally established early in life, but is modified through social roles and life experiences. Discuss some experiences of the later years that may affect an older person's self-concept and that may negatively influence their self-esteem.

3.   Cognitive appraisal has been suggested as a modifier of the perceived stressfulness of a life event. Other researchers have noted that life events are stressful by their very nature. Provide arguments supporting and opposing each position.

4.   Discuss the advantages and disadvantages of using a standard life events rating scale developed with younger persons in research with older persons.

5.   Describe the elements of "successful aging." How would you council a baby boomer in the best ways to prepare for a successful old age?

6.   In what ways, if any, is depression manifested in older people? What types of depression are most common in this group? Which therapeutic interventions appear to be most successful in treating these forms of late life depression?

7.   Discuss some of the new developments in research on dementia, especially the research on causes of Alzheimer's disease. What, if any, implications do these studies have for diagnosing and treating AD patients.

8. Discuss the range of therapeutic interventions that could be beneficial to Alzheimer's patients and to their family members.

9. Describe why alcoholism is often more difficult to detect in older people, and why therapeutic interventions are critical for older alcoholics.

10. Develop a mental health service delivery system that would best fit the needs of chronically mentally ill older people.

Multiple Choice

(E) 1. Erik Erikson's theory of personality is known as:

      a.   a trait theory
X   b.   a stage theory
      c.   a dialectical theory
      d.   a psychosexual theory

(M) 2. A major difference between Freud and personality theorists who focus on adult development is that Freud:
      a.   emphasized development throughout the life cycle
      b.   discouraged the view that development proceeds through specific stages
      c.   focused on psychosocial development
X   d.   suggests that personality is developed by adolescence

(M) 3. A theory of personality that emphasizes the importance of inner exploration in the later years has been advanced by:
      a.   Erik Erikson
      b.   Daniel Levinson
      c.   David Gutmann
X   d.   Carl Jung

(M) 4. Which of the following personality theorists does not state that there is decreased sex role stereotyping with aging?
X   a.   Costa
      b.   Jung
      c.   Neugarten
      d.   Gutmann

(M) 5. The Kansas City studies have revealed that aging is associated with:

      a.   increased extroversion
X   b.   greater differentiation
      c.   greater risk-taking
      d.   an increase in conservative beliefs

(M) 6. Which of the following theories or models of personality development does not take a dialectical approach?
X   a.   Jung's
      b.   Erikson's
      c.   Levinson's
      d.   Riegel's

(E) 7. Which of the following is not one of the factors in Costa and McCrae's model?

          a.   neuroticism
X   b.   inferiority
          c.   agreeableness
          d.   conscientiousness

(M) 8. Martha prefers to read and spend time by herself, rather than attending social functions. In Costa and McCrai's model, Martha would be considered low on the dimension of:
          a.   neuroticism
X   b.   extraversion
          c.   openness to experience
          d.   agreeableness

(M) 9. John has been described by his family as lazy, careless, unenergetic, and aimless. He would be considered low on Costa and McCrae's dimension of:
          a.   neuroticism
          b.   openness to experience
          c.   agreeableness
X   d.   conscientiousness

(M) 10. Research on Costa and McCrae's model of personality traits shows:

          a.   little evidence of stability
          b.   stability for only a few years
X   c.   strong support for long-term stability
          d.   no support for trait theories

(M) 11. Older people whose self-concept is closely associated with the roles they held when younger:
          a.   generally adjust more readily to aging
X   b.   usually have more difficulty adapting to aging
          c.   cope well with off-time events
          d.   have higher self-esteem than other older people

(M) 12. Compared to younger persons who have not experienced a particular life event, older people who have experienced that event:
          a.   assign a higher readjustment score to the event
X   b.   assign it a lower readjustment score
          c.   report that it was not at all stressful
          d.   report using multiple coping responses to it.

(E) 13. All of the following may determine older people's reaction to a life event <u>except</u>:

    a.   their cognitive appraisal of the situation
    b.   the availability of a strong social network
X   c.   chronological age
    d.   locus of control

(E) 14. Adults are more likely than children to use the defense mechanism of:

    a.   denial
    b.   projection
    c.   reminiscence
X   d.   sublimation

(M) 15. Older people who age successfully have been found to have all the following characteristics <u>except</u>:
X   a.   continuation of paid employment
    b.   independence in ADL's
    c.   high on cognitive abilities
    d.   active involvement with society

(C) 16. Successful or robust aging implies that the older person:

    a.   has reached at least age 85
    b.   has achieved ego integrity
X   c.   feels a sense of purpose
    d.   uses health services more than average

(M) 17. Which of the following is not part of DSM-IV criteria for depression?

    a.   dysphoria
    b.   length of time symptoms have been present
X   c.   excessive worry
    d.   physical symptoms

(M) 18. An important symptom that must be evaluated carefully in older adults who complain of feeling depressed is:

    a.   dysphoria
    b.   low energy
    c.   memory complaints
X   d.   apathy

(M) 19. The most common form of depression in the later years is:

        a.   bipolar depression
X   b.   unipolar depression
        c.   grief reaction
        d.   reactive depression

(M) 20. It is often difficult to diagnose depression in older people because:

        a.   they show no symptoms
        b.   they are more likely to complain of mood changes
X   c.   they are more likely to have somatic and memory complaints
        d.   they do not believe in the value of medical interventions for depression

(M) 21. The least effective therapy for older depressed persons is:

X   a.   to do nothing
        b.   antidepressant medications
        c.   ECT
        d.   psychotherapy

(M) 22. Suicide rates among different age and ethnic groups, and between men and women,:

        a.   do not vary widely
        b.   are highest in young males, lowest in white females
X   c.   are highest among older white males, lowest in non-white females
        d.   are highest among older Black males, lowest among white females

(M) 23. Older people are more likely than younger people to:

        a.   discuss but never complete a suicide attempt
X   b.   successfully carry out a suicide
        c.   seek psychiatric help to prevent a suicide
        d.   provide many cues about an impending suicide

(M) 24. Dementia in old age:

        a.   is a natural accompaniment to the aging process
        b.   generally is irreversible
X   c.   should first be examined for reversible causes
        d.   most often manifests itself as a personality disorder

(M) 25. The diagnosis of Alzheimer's disease:

          a.   is straightforward because of distinctive symptoms
          b.   can be made most accurately through psychological testing
          c.   is different from any other form of dementia
X   d.   is most accurate at autopsy

(M) 26. There is considerable research evidence currently to conclude that most forms of Alzheimer's disease are caused by:

          a.   a chromosomal defect
          b.   an accumulation of aluminum in the brain
          c.   a slow virus
X   d.   high levels of abnormal proteins in the brain

(M) 27. The region in the brain that appears to show the first signs of plaques and tangles is the _____; this is associated with early stage changes in _____ among Alzheimer's patients.

X   a.   hippocampus/learning and memory
          b.   locus ceruleus/anger
          c.   cerebral cortex/language
          d.   limbic system/movement

(M) 28. As the stress of caregiving has become increasingly recognized, which of the following has not emerged as a way to assist caregivers?

          a.   support groups
          b.   the ADRDA
X   c.   Medicare reimbursement for caregivers' psychotherapy
          d.   adult day care centers

(M) 29. Compared to younger persons, people over age 65:

          a.   are more likely to abuse drugs and alcohol
X   b.   are more likely to take prescription and over-the-counter drugs
          c.   are more likely to seek psychiatric help for alcoholism
          d.   are less likely to be affected by multiple medications

(M) 30. The chronically mentally ill population:

X   a.   suffers from social disruption
          b.   includes very few elderly
          c.   consists of long-term drug addicts
          d.   gets regular psychotherapy

(M) 31. For which of the following people is ECT <u>not</u> recommended?

         a.   older adults with heart disease
         b.   people who are suicidal
X   c.   individuals with mild depression
         d.   people with whom drugs do not work

(M) 32. A type of therapy that emphasizes changing maladaptive beliefs is

         a.   psychoanalytic therapy
         b.   behavioral therapy
X   c.   cognitive therapy
         d.   drug therapy

(E) 33. Hypertension is a risk factor for:

         a.   Creutzfeld-Jakob disease
X   b.   Multi-infarct dementia
         c.   Alzheimer's disease
         d.   Parkinson's

(C) 34. Recent studies of Alzheimer's disease have found that a preventive strategy for older women might be:
X   a.   estrogen replacement
         b.   active social involvement
         c.   physical exercise
         d.   treatment of depression

True or False

(M) 1. Most people experience maladaptive personality shifts as they age.

   True _____   False _X_

(M) 2. Socialization into old age is easy for most people because of the widespread availability of successful role models.

   True _____   False _X_

(E) 3. Both men and women move toward greater interiority as they age.

   True _X_   False _____

(E) 4. Differences in readjustment scores assigned to the same life event by people who have and have not experienced the event suggest that the anticipation of many events may be more stressful than their actual occurrence.

   True _X_   False _____

(M) 5. There is considerable research evidence that most normative events, such as the death of one's spouse in old age, result in less stress than non-normative events.

   True _____   False _X_

(M) 6. Defense mechanisms and coping strategies may both be defined as unconscious means of adapting to stressful situations.

   True _____   False _X_

(M) 7. Levinson's "life structures" are analogous to Erikson's stages of ego development.

   True _____   False _X_

(M) 8. Major longitudinal studies of successful aging have generally found that even this group of older people have multiple chronic diseases.

   True _____   False _X_

(E) 9. Adaptation to old age is easier for those with good coping skills.

   True _X_   False _____

(M) 10. Depression in older people generally cannot be treated as well as depression in younger persons.

   True _____   False _X_

(M) 11. Recent statistics reveal a significant increase in suicide rates among older African American men.

   True _____   False _X_

(E) 12. Older white men who are widowed, age 85+, with chronic pain and depression are at greatest risk for suicide.

True _X_   False ___

(M) 13. Older people using multiple medications may, as a result, develop an irreversible dementia.

True ___   False _X_

(M) 14. There is a significant difference between senile and presenile dementia in their symptoms and course.

True ___   False _X_

(M) 15. Family caregivers of older people with Alzheimer's disease are at a greater risk for depression and cardiovascular disease than age-matched non-caregivers..

True _X_   False ___

(M) 16. It is important to thoroughly screen patients with symptoms of dementia so that treatment for potentially reversible causes may be initiated.

True _X_   False ___

(E) 17. Alcoholism is higher among older men than among middle-aged men.

True ___   False _X_

(M) 18. Older persons are far less likely to seek care from a psychiatrist than from their family doctor for psychiatric symptoms.

True _X_   False ___

(E) 19. Noncompliance with pharmacotherapy is less common among older persons than among younger patients.

True ___   False _X_

(E) 20. Chronically mentally ill older persons receive good medical care because local hospitals keep track of most of these people.

True ___   False _X_

CHAPTER 7: LOVE, INTIMACY, AND SEXUALITY IN OLD AGE

Glossary

Climacteric

Erection

Estrogen

Gay

Heterosexuality

Homosexuality

Hot Flashes

Hysterectomy

Impotence

Intimacy

Lesbian

Male Menopause

Mastectomy

Masturbation

Topics for Discussion

1.   What are the prevalent attitudes and beliefs about sex and love in old age? Discuss ways that these are reflected in our society and what consequences they have for older adults.

2.   What are the major factors that affect sexual activity in older adults?

3.   Discuss the primary physiological changes that are experienced by men and women and the implications for sexual response, performance and pleasure.

4.   How can professionals assist older men and women to adapt to age-related changes that will enhance their experiences with intimacy and their sexual functioning and enjoyment?

5.   In what ways do nursing homes deny the sexuality of residents? What can nursing home staff do to respect the sexual needs of older residents?

6.   What are particular issues that older gay men and lesbians face in our society? If you were a health care professional, how would you try to address these issues in working with older homosexual couples?

7.   Discuss reasons why new drugs to treat impotence are selling so quickly? What does this reflect about societal norms and expectations regarding men's sexuality.

Multiple Choice

(C) 1. The early research on sexuality of older adults was limited in all of the following ways <u>except</u> for:
- a. an emphasis on frequency of sexual intercourse
- b. the nonrepresentative nature of samples
- c. comparisons of younger and older cohorts
- X d. longitudinal research designs

(M) 2. The climacteric is:

- a. a medicine for treating sexual dysfunction
- X b. a decline in sexual hormone levels resulting in a loss or reduction of reproductive ability.
- c. a hormone
- d. a stage of sexual functioning

(E) 3. In old age, sexual feelings:

- a. continue only if they are acted upon
- X b. can be expressed in ways other than genital contact
- c. are inappropriate
- d. normally fade away

(M) 4. Which of the following physiological conditions are related to the decrease in estrogen in menopausal and postmenopausal women:

- a. hot flashes
- b. genital atrophy
- c. urinary tract changes
- d. bone changes
- X e. all of the above

(M) 5. A woman's experience with menopause is influenced by:

- a. loss of estrogen
- b. the meaning a woman attaches to the loss of her ability to reproduce
- c. her personality
- X d. all of the above
- e. none of the above

(M) 6. When health care providers discuss sexuality with older people, they need to:

      a.   address the physiological changes that may affect sexual functioning
      b.   take account of the older person's attitudes and beliefs relating to sexuality
      c.   be sensitive to the meaning of intimacy to the older person
X   d.   all of the above
      e.   none of the above

(M) 7. A recent positive change in the treatment of menopause is:

      a.   use of prescription drugs
X   b.   the increased use of nonmedical or naturopathic approaches and social support
      c.   use of estrogen
      d.   none of the above
      e.   all of the above

(C) 8. Which of the following is true?

      a.   Older males enjoy sex more than older females.
X   b.   The male climacteric comes later and progresses at a slower rate than the female climacteric.
      c.   Women's capacity for orgasm is severely impaired after the age of 65.
      d.   none of the above

(M) 9. Which of the following is true about older lesbians?

      a.   They are less fearful of changes in appearance than heterosexual women.
      b.   Most remain sexually active as they age.
      c.   They usually report a positive self-image.
X   d.   all of the above
      e.   none of the above

(M) 10. Which of the following is not true about older gay men?

      a.   They are more concerned about their physical appearance than are lesbians.
      b.   They generally maintain positive feelings about their looks.
X   c.   Most are lonely and depressed.
      d.   all of the above

(C) 11. Which of the following conditions are common causes of impotence in older males?

       a.   prolonged alcoholism
       b.   diabetes
       c.   arthritis
X   d.   a and b
       e.   a and c

(M) 12. The primary cause of older men's withdrawing from sexual activity is:

       a.   lack of orgasm
       b.   fear of failure
X   c.   impotence
       d.   all of the above

(C) 13. Aging alters men's sexual functioning by:

       a.   making them impotent
       b.   creating a loss of interest in sexual activity
       c.   reducing the time between orgasm and subsequent erection
X   d.   increasing the time between orgasm and subsequent erection

(M) 14. Which of the following is true?

       a.   Little sexual pleasure is possible for males with irreversible impotence.
X   b.   A major barrier for older women to be sexually active is lack of a partner.
       c.   Tranquilizers heighten sexual performance.
       d.   Older men ejaculate more quickly.

(M) 15. Which of the following chronic illnesses can affect sexuality?

       a.   Arthritis
       b.   Diabetes
       c.   Medication
       d.   All of the above
       e.   None of the above

(E) 16. In instances where an older person conveys concern about his/her sexuality to a health care provider, which of the following is <u>not</u> an appropriate professional response?

       a.   Determine whether drugs are affecting sexual performance
X   b.   Tell the older person that he/she should no longer worry about sexual responsiveness
       c.   Screen for any disease-related causes of changes in sexual responsiveness

(M) 17. Which of the following statements about sexual activity in late adulthood is true?

        a.   The major barrier for men is lack of a partner.
        b.   There are physiological limits to how long women can be sexually active.
X   c.   The most important factor in maintaining sexuality is consistent sexual activity throughout middle and late adulthood.
        d.   all of the above
        e.   none of the above

(M) 18. Widower's syndrome is a condition that may occur in older males who:

X   a.   have refrained from sexual activity for an extended period of time following their wife's death
        b.   have intense and frequent sexual activity following their wife's death
        c.   are terrified of their wife's death
        d.   none of the above

(M) 19. Sexual expression can assume more significance in old age if:

        a.   nursing homes provide privacy
        b.   doctors avoid prescribing drugs that interfere with sexuality
        c.   younger people do not ridicule older people's sexual feelings
X   d.   all of the above

(M) 20. Sexuality refers to:

        a.   an energy force expressed in every aspect of being
        b.   a person's speech, movement, vitality and ability to enjoy life
        c.   the expression of feelings and self in an intimate way
X   d.   all of the above

(M) 21. When visiting an older person in a nursing home, the most important type of sensory stimulation that a visitor might provide is:

        a.   wearing bright colored clothing
X   b.   touching the older person (such as backrubs, holding hands)
        c.   feeding the older person
        d.   wearing cologne

True or False

(E) 1. Sexuality often continues to be an important part of relationships in late adulthood.
        True <u>X</u>   False ___

(E) 2. The majority of older adults do not engage in sexual intercourse.
        True ___   False <u>X</u>

(M) 3. Reanalysis of the 1954 Duke Longitudinal Study data found older women to be more interested in sex than older men.
        True <u>X</u>   False ___

(C) 4. Recent research suggests that men do not experience significant hormonal changes as they age.
        True ___   False <u>X</u>

(E) 5. Physiological, age-related changes can affect the nature of the sexual response.
        True <u>X</u>   False ___

(E) 6. The majority of older women experience only mild menopausal symptoms.
        True <u>X</u>   False ___

(M) 7. Only a very small percentage of women experience hot flashes during menopause.
        True ___   False <u>X</u>

(E) 8. The majority of older women experience and enjoy orgasms.
        True <u>X</u>   False ___

(M) 9. Prostate surgery does not always result in irreversible impotence.
        True <u>X</u>   False ___

(M) 10. The only treatment for prostate cancer is a form of surgery called radical prostatectomy.
        True ___   False <u>X</u>

(M) 11. Impotence, the most common sexual disorder among older men, is sometimes caused by psychological factors.
        True <u>X</u>   False ___

(E) 12. Frail nursing home residents have little need for sexual intimacy.
        True ___   False <u>X</u>

(E) 13. Sex therapy with older adults should emphasize ways to maintain genital intercourse.
        True ___   False <u>X</u>

(M) 14. During late adulthood, sex and love are more important than at any other time of life.

        True ___   False_X

(E) 15. The major barrier to older women's sexual activity is the availability of a partner.

        True _X_   False ___

CHAPTER 8: SOCIAL THEORIES OF AGING

Glossary

Activity Theory
Age Stratification Theory
Cohort
Continuity Theory
Critical Theory
Disengagement Theory
Feminist Perspective
Interactionist Perspective
Labeling Theory
Life Course Perspective

Opportunity Structures
Political Economy of Aging
Positivism
Postmodern Theory
Role Theory
Social Exchange Theory
Social Phenomenology and
    Constructionism
Structural Lag
Subculture Theory
Symbolic Interactionism

Topics for Discussion

1.   List several ways that an older person may act that are contrary to expectations of behavior by chronological age (age norms). What often happens when an older individual violates age norms?

2.   Debate the question: Do older people constitute a distinct subculture?

3.   Which theory in this chapter is most consistent with your own view of aging? What evidence supports this theory?

4.   Which theory described in this chapter could provide you with useful guidelines for working with older people in community based settings? Give examples of practice guidelines that you could derive from this particular theoretical perspective.

5.   What common themes do you see in the ways that both older people and our social institutions attempt to deal with the issue of dependency?

6.   According to Sharon Curtin in <u>Nobody Ever Died of Old Age</u>, "There is nothing to prepare you for the experience of growing old." Based upon the theoretical perspectives in this chapter, how would you advise younger adults to prepare for this experience? How will you approach your own aging?

7.   What theories are reflected in current social policies toward older people? How can exchange theory be used to justify reductions in services and benefits for older people?

8.   Based upon what you know about critical theory and a feminist perspective, explain why women in old age tend to have fewer economic resources than men.

Multiple Choice

(C) 1. Social theories of aging over time differ from earlier theories in the following ways:

        a.   more focus on the individual factors
        b.   less focus on structural factors
X   c.   attempts to understand the meaning of age-related changes for those sequencing them
        d.   greater reliance on the positivist scientific tradition

(M) 2. Social theories of aging address the basic question of:

X   a.   the optimal way for older people to adapt
        b.   how older people socialize
        c.   older people's needs vis-a-vis family interactions
        d.   the impact of physiological changes on older people

(M) 3. Which of the following is true concerning changes in roles that occur with age?

        a.   Role losses tend to occur more frequently.
        b.   Role losses can lead to a decline in self esteem.
        c.   Role gains are impossible .
        d.   all of the above.
X   e.   a & b

(E) 4. Growing old may imply some new kinds of dependency on others. In working with an older person, which one of the approaches listed below would help him or her accept such dependency with dignity?

        a.   draw their attention to all the roles they have lost
X   b.   create a sense of giving and receiving in their relationships
        c.   help them deny their losses and act as if nothing has happened
        d.   remind them that all older people lose power as they age and that they aren't so bad off

(E) 5. A theory that is consistent with society's values of work and productivity is:

        a.   cognitive-behavioral theory
X   b.   activity theory
        c.   continuity theory
        d.   role theory

(C) 6. One of the major limitations of activity theory is:

    a. It fails to acknowledge the role of personality.
    b. It defines aging as an individual problem.
    c. It assumes that older people are able to continue the activities of middle age.
    d. none of the above
X   e. all of the above.

(E) 7. The theory that is based on the idea that an elder's value depends on the balance of his/her contributions against the cost of supporting him/her is called:

    a. disengagement theory
    b. activity theory
X   c. social exchange theory
    d. continuity theory

(M) 8. The life course perspective on aging:

    a. views development as steady incremental growth
    b. focuses only on individual change
X   c. takes account of variation in roles and role changes over time
    d. none of the above

(E) 9. The theory that proposes that people seek more passive social roles and interact less frequently with others as they age is called:

    a. cognitive
    b. activity
    c. social reconstruction
X   d. disengagement

(C) 10. A major limitation of activity theory and disengagement theory is that:

    a. they both focus on healthy older people only
    b. they both focus on the best way to age
X   c. neither addresses the historical, social, structural or cultural contexts of aging
    d. neither addresses the biological context of aging

(E) 11. One of the shortcomings of disengagement theory is:

    a. it assumes that older people identify only with one another
    b. it assumes that people maintain typical ways of adjusting to the environment as they age
    c. it assumes that older adults are discriminated against because of their age
X   d. it assumes that withdrawal from social roles is functional and experienced as desirable by most older people

(E) 12. The theory based on the assumption that people have basic core personality characteristics that remains fairly stable throughout adulthood and old age is:

    a. disengagement
X   b. continuity
    c. exchange
    d. role

(C) 13. Symbolic interactionism, labeling theory and the subculture of aging are all characterized by:
    a. the importance of the role of personality in how an individual ages
    b. the inevitability of social withdrawal by older people
    c. the continuity of behavior over time
X   d. the dynamic interaction between older people and their social environments
    e. none of the above

(M) 14. A basic assumption of age stratification theory is:

    a. every society is stratified in terms of socioeconomic class.
    b. older persons form an age strata because of their age-based consciousness.
X   c. age is a universal criterion by which people's roles, rights, and rewards are distributed.
    d. the factors of life course dimension and historical dimension explain similarities in people's behaviors and attitudes.

(C) 15. The dynamic nature of age stratification is exemplified by:

    a. successive cohorts change how aging is viewed
    b. as current cohorts age, they alter the aging experience for future cohorts
    c. social structures cannot keep pace with the changes in an aging population
X   d. all of the above
    e. none of the above

(E) 16. Which theory states that people age most successfully by remaining involved in as many roles as possible and finding substitutes for lost roles?

    a.   continuity

X   b.   activity

    c.   disengagement

    d.   integrity

(E) 17. Which of the following assumptions are fundamental to the social exchange theory of aging?

    a.   power or the control of valued resources

    b.   Older adults have limited access to valued resources compared to younger people

    c.   Dependence and deference characterize the interactions of many older people

    d.   Most people try to maintain some reciprocity in their interactions

X   e.   all of the above

(M) 18. Which of the following types of changes refer to the events in society experienced by groups of people born at approximately the same time?

    a.   age-graded

X   b.   cohort flow

    c.   unique

    d.   none of the above

(C) 19. The political economy perspective maintains that:

    a.   on the basis of their shared experiences with discrimination, older people have developed a cohesive subculture.

X   b.   structural factors have defined older adults as a problem to be solved.

    c.   older individuals tend to withdraw from the labor market, which is beneficial to the economy.

    d.   social policy has sought to make fundamental changes in the conditions of older people.

    e.   all of the above

(M) 20. Social phenomenology and social constructionism are characterized by:

    a.   their use of quantitative methods

    b.   systematic efforts to explain how individuals age

    c.   their focus on social structure and power

X   d.   their attempt to understand the meaning of aging

    e.   all of the above

(C) 21. A critical theorist would approach aging as

         a.   a model based on social problems facing older people

X   b.   a multidimensional, diverse process defined by older people themselves

         c.   a problem to be measured empirically

         d.   all of the above

         e.   none of the above

(C) 22. The issues of caregiving in old age are defined by feminist theorists as

         a.   a growing social problem

         b.   an issue that can be addressed by women asking their relatives to assist them more with caregiving tasks

X   c.   an example of women's unequal access to power throughout their lives

         d.   a growing private responsibility

True or False

(M) 1. Social theories of aging have been adequately tested so that we are able to predict with considerable accuracy the behavior of older individuals.
      True ____   False_X_

(E) 2. Scientific theories serve as a guide to further research.
      True _X_   False ____

(E) 3. Most empirical research on disengagement theory fails to support it.
      True _X_   False ____

(E) 4. In social exchange theory, when one person is dependent upon another, the latter achieves power.
      True _X_   False ____

(M) 5. According to social exchange theory, older people disengage from society because it is beneficial both to themselves and to society.
      True ____   False_X_

(E) 6. According to disengagement theory, people age most successfully if they withdraw from active involvement in society.
      True _X_   False ____

(C) 7. One of the implications of the political economy perspective is the need to develop more medical services for older adults.
      True ____   False_X_

(M) 8. The political economy perspective examines the larger sociopolitical conditions that underlie current policies and practices toward the older population.
      True _X_   False ____

(E) 9. Socialization into old age is easy for most people because of the widespread availability of positive role models.
      True ____   False_X_

(M) 10. The most recent theoretical developments in social aging build on the positivist tradition.
      True ____   False_X_

(M) 11. The symbolic interactionist view of aging takes account of the meaning of a particular activity within the older person's environment.
      True _X_   False ____

(C) 12. The subculture of aging perspective believes that older people derive their self-concept from how others define and react to them.

    True ___   False_X

(C) 13. The life span perspective in particularly useful for understanding the power relationships involved in family caregiving.

    True ___   False_X

CHAPTER 9: THE IMPORTANCE OF SOCIAL SUPPORTS: FAMILY, FRIENDS, AND NEIGHBORS

Glossary

Blended Family
Caregiving
Caregiver Burden
Case Management
Elder Abuse
Elder Neglect
Empty Nest
Extended Family
Family and Medical Leave Act
Filial Responsibility
Gatekeepers
Grandparents as Editors
Grandparent's Rights
Women in the Middle

Intergenerational Living
Intergenerational Programming
Intergenerational Transfer of
   Knowledge
Intimacy at a Distance
Multigenerational Family
Natural Helpers
Non-traditional Families
Reciprocal Support
Sandwich Generation
Social Support
*Formal
*Informal

Topics for Discussion

1.   What do you think are some factors that explain the persistence of myths about the aging family in our culture?

2.   You have been asked to recommend policies and programs regarding family caregiving to your state legislature. Based upon the evidence regarding families' needs, what policy and programmatic changes would you recommend? What would be the rationale for your recommendations?

3.   What are some steps that you could take now to ensure that you will have a strong informal support system in old age?

4.   What are some of the social and cultural factors that underlie why family caregivers of older adults (especially spouses) have tended to be ignored by practitioners and policy makers?

5.   Assume that you are the director of a retirement home where most residents are age 75 and over. What programs might you develop to foster intergenerational contacts?

6.   Assume that you are a counselor working with a four-generation family which is experiencing conflicts over caring for a great-grandparent. What would you do to encourage positive intergenerational exchanges? Specifically, what could be done to strengthen the grandchildren-grandparent interactions?

7.   From the perspective of your discipline, describe an intervention(s) to strengthen an older person's social support system within a high rise apartment building for low-income elders.

8.   What kinds of services and supports would you recommend for the growing numbers of grandparents who are assuming the primary care of grandchildren?

9.   Discuss how ethnic minority status, socioeconomic class, gender and sexual orientation affect family roles and relationships for older people.

10.   In what ways is the aging family of the future likely to be different from contemporary families? What are the major factors that are likely to change the structure of older families in the future?

11.   If you were designing a training program on diversity for community home health care staff, what content would you include about families, including gay and lesbian partners?

(M) 1. The growth of the multigenerational family is due to:

X   a.   an increase in life expectancy
        b.   higher fertility
        c.   later child bearing
        d.   all of the above
        e.   none of the above

(M) 2. Which of the following statements about the aging family is true?

        a.   Most older persons live so geographically distant from their families that they do not regularly see any relatives.
X   b.   Family members provide the majority of in-home care to older relatives with functional disabilities.
        c.   At the turn of the century, the majority of older people lived in multigenerational households.
        d.   Most older people would prefer to live with their children and grandchildren.

(M) 3. In terms of living situation, most older adults live:
        a.   in institutions
        b.   alone
X   c.   with a spouse, partner, children or other relatives
        d.   with non-relatives

(C) 4. Studies of marital satisfaction across the lifespan show that marital satisfaction:

        a.   decreases with length of time married
        b.   decreases when children are being reared, and gets lower when children leave home
X   c.   is high among those recently married, lower during the childrearing period, and higher in later phases of the marriage
        d.   is high among those recently married and is lower when children leave home

(M) 5. Although research on older gay and lesbian partners is limited, we can conclude with reasonable certainty that:

        a.   they are more satisfied in old age than their heterosexual peers.
        b.   they are more concerned with physical appearance than their heterosexual peers.
X   c.   they face certain structural and legal barriers not encountered by their heterosexual peers.
        d.   all of the above

(E) 6. The strongest sibling relationships are usually between:
   a. brothers
X b. sisters
   c. brothers and sisters
   d. oldest and youngest siblings

(M) 7. Studies of older siblings indicate that:

   a. contacts among siblings are more frequent than among other relationships.
   b. few older persons have siblings alive.
   c. contact is greatest in middle age and then declines.
X d. feelings of affection and closeness often increase with age.

(M) 8. There are many different myths about the aging family. Which of the following is not a myth, but instead a true statement?

   a. Most older adults have little contact with family members.
X b. Most older people prefer not to live with their children, but instead like "intimacy at a distance."
   c. Older individuals usually become alienated from their children.
   d. Most families place their older relatives in nursing homes.

(E) 9. The primary source of emotional support for an older person generally is:

   a. neighbors
   b. clergy
X c. family
   d. friends

(M) 10. Patterns of assistance among members of the multigenerational family are affected by:

   a. women's increased labor force participation
   b. geographic mobility of younger family members
   c. growing rates of divorce and remarriage
   d. the growth of frail older people
X e. all of the above.

(M) 11. Studies of relationships between adult children and their older parents indicate:

X a. most older parents see an adult child frequently
   b. most parents do not live geographically near to any of their children.
   c. most older parents are alienated from their children.
   d. most older parents rarely see their children.

(M) 12. Women compose nearly _____% of the primary family caregivers for older relatives with chronic illness.
    a.   30
    b.   50
X   c.   80
    d.   none of the above

(C) 13. Older people who never married and are without children, and thus do not have adult children to care for them, are characterized as follows:
    a.   generally are more destitute than those with children
X   b.   usually develop other support systems and turn to others for help
    c.   are often much happier because adult children tend to let down their older parents
    d.   generally experience much worse health

(M) 14. The "sandwiched generation" is typically:

    a.   middle aged
    b.   responsible for providing care to at least two generations of dependents
    c.   juggling the roles of paid worker and caregiver to dependents
X   d.   all of the above
    e.   none of the above

(M) 15. The greatest burdens experienced by family caregivers to older persons are:

    a.   the costs of medical care
    b.   the physical demands of cooking and cleaning
X   c.   the emotional burdens of feeling alone and without time for oneself
    d.   the feeling that they are doing more than they should be

(M) 16. Middle-aged adult children are experiencing growing pressures to provide care to their older parents because:
    a.   the current cohort of older adults had fewer children than previous generations'
    b.   the proportion of people age 85+ has grown more rapidly than any other age group
    c.   most families try to avoid nursing home placement for as long as possible
X   d.   all of the above
    e.   none of the above

(M) 17. The primary responsibility for meeting the needs of aging parents generally falls upon:

    a.   the oldest members of the family
    b.   the family member with the most money
X   c.   female members of the family
    d.   both sexes equally

(C) 18. Families' use of social and health services can be characterized as follows:

          a.   families turn readily to formal services
          b.   once services are available, families withdraw from providing care
X   c.   families use services selectively to supplement their own caregiving
          d.   none of the above.

(C) 19. Parents of adult children who are developmentally disabled or chronically mentally ill can be characterized as:

          a.   generally lacking adequate services to plan for their child's well-being
          b.   facing their own age-related changes
          c.   perpetual caregivers
X.   d.   all of the above
          e.   none of the above

(M) 20. Neglect or physical or psychological abuse of older family members is:

X   a.   most likely to be committed by a spouse who is the primary caregiver or by a son
          b.   probably over-reported
          c.   present in nearly all multigenerational families
          d.   all of the above

(M) 21. The following factor(s) have been found to increase the probability of elder abuse:

          a.   substance abuse
          b.   aggressive behavior on the part of the older person
          c.   dementia in the older person
          d.   none of the above
X   e.   all of the above

(C) 22. It is estimated that _____ of older adults in the United States are victims of abuse or neglect.
X   a.   3% to 4%
          b.   8%
          c.   10%
          d.   12%

(C) 23. A major predictor of nursing home placement is:

          a.   the nature of the older person's illness
          b.   the older person's mental competence
          c.   the condition of the older person's home
X   d.   the family caregiver's physical and mental status and social supports

(C) 24. The primary factor that affects the frequency of visiting between grandparents and grandchildren is:

X   a.   geographic proximity
       b.   the gender of the grandparent and grandchild
       c.   whether or not parents and grandparents get along with one another
       d.   divorce

(M) 25. Friendship patterns in later life appear to be most strongly related to:

       a.   the type of assistance needed
       b.   similarity in terms of age and other characteristics
       c.   gender
       d.   length of neighborhood residence
X   e.   all of the above
       f.   none of the above

(M) 26. In their social relationships in later life, men tend to:

       a.   place more value on friendships than women do
       b.   be more aggressive about their friendships than women are
X   c.   depend on their wives for companionship
       d.   have a greater need for friends in later life than women do

(M) 27. Interventions with informal support systems aim to:

       a.   strengthen natural helping networks
       b.   enhance a group or community's problem-solving capacity
       c.   build upon natural helpers' interactions with older people
       d.   none of the above
X   e.   all of the above

(M) 28. In recent years, ethnic minority families have experienced the following:

       a.   increasing intergenerational solidarity over time
X   b.   weakening of the extended family in urban settings
       c.   less stress from caregiving than Caucasian families
       d.   all of the above
       e.   none of the above

True or False

(M) 1. Surveys have found that older persons who are the most satisfied are those who are married.

   True _X_   False ___

(E) 2. The largest category of single persons in the current cohort of older people is divorced persons.

   True ___   False _X_

(M) 3. Childless older adults with health problems tend to be more isolated than other older people are.

   True _X_   False ___

(E) 4. Divorce in later life is decreasing.

   True ___   False _X_

(E) 5. In terms of the proportion of older men and women who are married, there is a higher percentage of older married men than women.

   True _X_   False ___

(E) 6. Older men who are divorced have the least chance of remarriage.

   True ___   False _X_

(M) 7. The majority of older individuals live alone.

   True ___   False _X_

(M) 8. Having common interests and values is the most important factor in successful marriage in late adulthood.

   True _X_   False ___

(E) 9. Among siblings in old age, sisters are more likely to maintain family ties than are brothers.

   True _X_   False ___

(E) 10. Most studies indicate that the majority of adult children now reject the norm of filial responsibility (i.e., that adult children should help their parents).

   True ___   False _X_

(M) 11. Older parents typically receive help from their adult children but rarely are able to assist their children.

   True ___   False _X_

(M) 12. Multigenerational households tend to be more prevalent among ethnic minority families compared to Caucasian families.
       True <u>X</u>   False ___

(E) 13. Formal institutions, such as day care centers and nursing homes, now provide more care than does the family.
       True ___   False <u>X</u>

(E) 14. Most families prefer nursing home placements over trying to maintain their older relatives at home.
       True ___   False <u>X</u>

(M) 15. The role of grandparent tends to be the most important one in an older person's life.
       True ___   False <u>X</u>

(M) 16. The majority of older people are grandparents and see a grandchild at least once a week.
       True <u>X</u>   False ___

(M) 17. Friends are often a more important source of support than family in old age because they are chosen.
       True <u>X</u>   False ___

(M) 18. Informal support systems have been found to be more important to older adults' well-being than formal support services.
       True <u>X</u>   False ___

CHAPTER 10: LIVING ARRANGEMENTS AND SOCIAL INTERACTIONS

Glossary

Adult Day Care

Adult Foster Care

Assisted Living

Assistive Technology

Congregate Care

CCRC

Home Health Care

Homelessness

Long-Term Care

Medicaid Waivers

NORC

Nursing Homes

SRO Hotels

Topics for Discussion

1.   What aspects of person-environment congruence are most important in selecting housing for an older person who must relocate from his own home to a long-term care facility?

2.   Describe the advantages and disadvantages of suburban living for older people?

3.   Discuss some options available to an older person who does not wish to move to retirement housing, but prefers to stay in the large mortgage-free home in which she has lived for 40 years, but which she can no longer maintain.

4.   Describe Litwak and Longino's 3-stage model of migration among older people.

5.   Provide some guidelines for designing a multilevel facility for older people that would be suitable for a healthy and active 65-year-old, as well as for an 85-year-old with dementia.

6.   Discuss the pros and cons of assisted living facilities as an option for an older person who has problems with multiple ADLs.

7.   Describe the prevalence of crimes against older people, comparing by gender, race, and income level.

8.   Describe the impact of the loss of SRO housing on problems of homelessness among older Americans.

Multiple Choice

(M) 1. A person-environment perspective is useful for understanding human behavior because it assumes that:

     a. human behavior is consistent across settings
     b. people behave similarly in the same setting
X   c. behavior varies as a function of personal and environmental characteristics
     d. behavior cannot be changed by changing the physical environment

(E) 2. A model that examines person-environment relations vis-à-vis the older person's competence is that developed by:
X   a. Lawton & Nahemow
     b. Kahana
     c. French, Rodgers & Cobb
     d. Murray

(M) 3. Compared to younger age groups, people over age 65 are _____ likely to move to a different community and _____ likely to change housing types within the same community.
X   a. less/more
     b. less/less
     c. more/more
     d. more/less

(M) 4. Which of the following older groups is least likely to live in central cities?

X   a. middle class whites
     b. poor African Americans
     c. middle class Hispanic
     d. poor Asian Americans

(M) 5. Social interaction with young and old neighbors and friends is greatest for older people who live in:
     a. urban settings
     b. high rise apartments
X   c. small communities
     d. suburban tract housing

(M) 6. The 3-stage model of migration suggests that:

     a. after retirement, most Northeasterners move to the Sunbelt permanently
     b. older people prefer to move to their place of birth
X   c. major changes in health affect older people's relocation
     d. after retirement, most people move to a retirement apartment

(E) 7. The group that experiences the highest rates of victimization in all categories is the group that is aged:

X   a.   12 to 24
       b.   25 to 49
       c.   50 to 64
       d.   65 and older

(E) 8. Fear of crime is highest among older persons who:

       a.   live on isolated farms
X   b.   live in central cities
       c.   own their homes
       d.   are economically independent

(M) 9. Older people who have lived in their own home for many years and can no longer maintain them:
       a.   should move into special housing for elders
       b.   will be happiest if they can take in young renters
X   c.   are experiencing P-E incongruence
       d.   should take a reverse mortgage on their homes

(M) 10. Fear of crime among older women is least likely to be alleviated by:

       a.   "neighborhood watch" programs
       b.   education in self-defense
       c.   efforts to improve their environmental competence
X   d.   doing all of their errands during the day

(E) 11. Multilevel housing for older people:

       a.   means that the housing is most likely high rise apartments
       b.   always includes skilled nursing care
       c.   generally requires payment of a founder's fee
X   d.   allows movement to higher levels of care as needed

(M) 12. A person aged 65-74 with income > $25,000, and in a suburban community is most likely to live:
       a.   in a nursing home
       b.   in a rental home
X   c.   in his / her own house
       d.   with his / her own children

(M) 13. Housing that is owned by older people is more likely than that owned by younger people to:

X   a.   have structural and maintenance needs
         b.   have a large mortgage
         c.   be energy efficient
         d.   have a large number of related and unrelated residents

(M) 14. Regardless of the quality of an older person's own home, relocation is likely to occur if there are age-related changes in:

         a.   cognition
X   b.   health
         c.   social network
         d.   sensory functions

(E) 15. Older adults who have lived in the same place for decades, feel _____ to their neighborhoods.
         a.   dedicated
         b.   linked
         c.   animosity
X   d.   attachment

(M) 16. One aspect of older adults' housing that is often overlooked is that it is:

         a.   usually in better neighborhoods than young adults live in
         b.   typically not owned by the residents themselves
X   c.   often inappropriate for his / her changing needs
         d.   usually in poor apartment complexes

(M) 17. One of the most pressing housing needs in the United States is the need for more:

         a.   retirement communities
X   b.   affordable assisted living
         c.   age-segregated apartment complexes
         d.   age-integrated communities

(E) 18. Which of the following characteristics does not describe the typical nursing home resident?
         a.   middle class white
         b.   poor white
         c.   widowed
X   d.   ethnic minority

(M) 19. The chances of an older American being institutionalized at some time during his/her lifetime are:
- a.   almost 50%
- X   b.   above 25%
- c.   very low, less than 5%
- d.   we don't really know the chances

(M) 20. A disadvantage of assisted living as a long-term care option today is that:

- a.   it can only house well elderly
- b.   it costs more than nursing home care
- c.   health services are not provided
- X   d.   most states do not provide Medicaid waivers

(M) 21. Which of the following is not growing rapidly as a long-term care option for frail elders?
- X   a.   nursing homes
- b.   assisted living
- c.   adult family homes
- d.   home health care

(M) 22. Home health care has been found to be effective in:

- a.   preventing nursing home use altogether
- b.   reducing death rates among older people
- X   c.   curtailing the use of hospitals
- d.   keeping older people independent

(M) 23. A factor partially responsible for the increase in homelessness among older adults is:

- X   a.   closing of SRO hotels
- b.   a lack of congregate housing
- c.   a lack of nursing home beds
- d.   continuing care retirement communities with very expensive buy-in fees

(M) 24. Studies of homeless men have found that:
- a.   very few are over age 60
- X   b.   many who qualify for social services do not get them
- c.   most use medical services regularly
- d.   most are using medications prescribed by their doctor

78

True or False

(M) 1. The person-environment perspective is useful in gerontology because older people's ability to control their environment is often diminished.
        True _X_   False ___

(M) 2. Researchers have found that an oversupply of an environmental characteristic vis-à-vis an individual's needs is generally better for maintaining life satisfaction than is an undersupply.
        True ___   False _X_

(E) 3. The majority of ethnic minority elders today live in suburbs.
        True ___   False _X_

(E) 4. The majority of older people live in single family homes that they own.
        True _X_   False ___

(M) 5. Public housing for older people should be located near freeways in order to make it easier for them to reach a variety of services.
        True ___   False _X_

(M) 6. Congregate housing is better for many older people than private apartments because meals are more likely to be provided for residents on site.
        True _X_   False ___

(E) 7. Many national surveys have revealed that fear of crime is a greater concern for many older people than their concerns about income or health status.
        True _X_   False ___

(M) 8. Assisted living is an excellent housing option for older people of all income levels.
        True ___   False _X_

(C) 9. With the growth of adult family homes, many older people with significant ADL impairments are being placed inappropriately in these facilities.
        True _X_   False ___

(M) 10. The proportion of older persons in nursing homes at any one time is higher in the U.S. than in any other Western country.
        True ___   False _X_

(M) 11. Medicare currently does not reimburse fully the costs entailed by older people who are placed in adult day centers.
        True _X_   False ___

(M) 12. The major source of funding for adult family home residents is Medicare.

        True ___   False X

(M) 13. Federal and state accessibility codes have established standards that require buildings to be better designed in order to meet the special sensory and physical needs of older residents.

        True ___   False X

(E) 14. SRO housing is becoming scarcer as an option for low income older people in urban centers.

        True X   False ___

(E) 15. Assisted living has been shown to be appropriate for only a small proportion of older people

        True ___   False X

CHAPTER 11: PRODUCTIVE AGING: PAID AND NONPAID ROLES AND ACTIVITIES

Glossary

Age Discrimination in Employment Act (ADEA)
American Association of Retired Persons (AARP)
American Society on Aging (ASA)
Assets
Baby Boomers
Demographic Trends
Displaced Homemaker
Elder Hostel
ERISA
  (Employment Retirement Income Security Act)
Feminization of Poverty
Foster Grandparents Program
Gerontological Society of America (GSA)
Gray Panthers
Leisure
National Association of Retired Federal Employees (NARFE)
National Council of Senior Citizens (NCSC)
Older American Volunteer Program
Older Women's League (OWL)
Retired Senior Volunteer Program (RSVP)

Retirement
Socioeconomic Status
Senior Community Services
  Employment Program (SCSEP)
Senior Companion Program
Senior Learning Programs
Serial Retirement
Service Corps of Retired Executives
  (SCORE)
Silver-haired legislatures
Social Security
Supplemental Security Income (SSI)
Vesting of Pension Benefits

Topics for Discussion

1.   Discuss the concept of productive aging. What are ways that older people can continue to play meaningful roles in our society? What are barriers to such roles?

2.   How are changing demographic, economic and social patterns likely to influence the employment/retirement patterns of men and women in the next 10 to 15 years?

3.   If you were the Director of Personnel in a corporation that wanted to maximize older workers' skills, what steps would you recommend to your company (e.g., changes in policies, programs, benefits, etc.)?

4.   How would you explain the research findings that most people state that they would prefer to be employed, even though most choose to retire early?

5.   What are the primary barriers to the employment of older individuals? What are some strategies to overcome these barriers?

6.   In planning for or thinking about your own retirement, what factors do you consider to be most important? What would you like to do upon retirement? What steps can you take now to help you achieve your retirement goals?

7.   How would you respond to the argument by some politically conservative organizations that older adults are financially better off than any other age group in our society and are "greedy geezers"?

8.   Discuss the reasons that certain groups of older people are more likely to be living in poverty than others (e.g. groups defined by age, gender, ethnic minority status, living arrangements, type of occupation, etc.). What kinds of long-term changes are needed in order to reduce these pockets of poverty.

9.   Presuming that you were a director of a senior center that depends upon volunteers, what steps would you take to recruit and retain older people as volunteers?

10.   Think about how you spend your own leisure time now. What benefits do you derive from your current leisure activities? What kinds of leisure activities would you anticipate participating in when you are older? Would they represent a continuation of or a change from current activities?

11.   What are some of the major challenges facing senior centers in the 1990's? If you were a senior center director, what kinds of programmatic changes would you recommend to your board?

12.   How can churches better meet older adults' religious and spiritual needs? What are the barriers to their doing so?

13.   From your knowledge of local and national political events, do you perceive the older population as a powerful political constituency? If not, what factors prevent them from exerting the power of their numbers?

14.   Discuss the pros and cons of age-based organizations versus intergenerational alliances to influence legislation and influence the condition faced by various age groups.

Multiple Choice

(M) 1. The concept of productive aging refers to:
      a.   paid work
      b.   successful aging
X   c.   the variety of valuable roles that older people play
      d.   none of the above

(M) 2. Patterns of employment since the 1930's suggest that there has been:

      a.   an increase in the number of people over age 50 employed full-time
X   b.   a trend toward early retirement
      c.   a decrease in the number of people over age 50 employed part-time
      d.   none of the above

(M) 3. Increased longevity and changing employment patterns have resulted in:

X   a.   both men and women spending more years in retirement
      b.   a greater proportion of the life span devoted to one job
      c.   fewer women entering the work force
      d.   women not entering the work force until after childbearing is completed

(C) 4. The employment patterns of older workers are more likely than younger workers to be characterized by:
X   a.   part-time jobs
      b.   low or entry-level positions
      c.   high tech positions
      d.   all of the above

(M) 5. Which of the following are barriers to part-time employment?

      a.   Social Security limits on the amount that can be earned until age 70.
      b.   employers' resistance to the additional health care costs
      c.   employer policies against employees drawing partial pensions
X   d.   all of the above.
      e.   none of the above.

(C) 6. The apparent contradiction between more older people seeking employment after they have chosen early retirement can be explained by:

      a.   economic factors
      b.   a desire to feel productive
      c.   social needs
X   d.   all of the above
      e.   none of the above

(M) 7. Which of the following will not be a barrier to employment for future cohorts of older people?
  a. age discrimination
X b. mandatory retirement
  c. negative stereotypes
  d. lack of opportunities

(M) 8. In the 21st century, the workforce will be characterized by:

X a. more older people seeking employment
  b. more younger workers seeking employment
  c. wide availability of higher paying full time positions
  d. none of the above

(E) 9. Which of the following is a false description of retirement?

  a. Retirement is a social institution.
X b. Retirement is a time of inevitable physical decline and poor health.
  c. Retirement is a process.
  d. Retirement is an opportunity for personal growth and learning new roles.

(E) 10. The primary factor that affect when a worker will retire is:

  a. the amount of retirement preparation
  b. the type of job
  c. his/her attitude toward leisure
X d. having an adequate retirement income

(M) 11. The retirement process for older ethnic minorities can be described as:

  a. similar to white retirees
X b. a blurring of the line between work and nonwork
  c. a time of economic security and good health
  d. none of the above

(C) 12. Early retirement is likely to occur when a person has:

  a. good health and an adequate retirement income
X b. poor health and an adequate retirement income
  c. poor health
  d. none of the above

(C) 13. From the perspective of social phenomenologists, retirement satisfaction is influenced by:

X   a.   how an individual experiences retirement and the meaning they attach to it

        b.   whether they have been adequately prepared

        c.   whether they can continue activities enjoyed prior to retirement

        d.   the support of their family and friends

(M) 14. From the perspective of continuity theory:

        a.   good health contributes to retirement satisfaction

        b.   adequate income influences one's retirement satisfaction

X   c.   one's self-esteem and satisfaction prior to retirement influence how one feels about retirement

        d.   all of the above

(M) 15. Which of the following factors is most important for good adjustment during retirement?

        a.   a person's place of residence

        b.   a person's gender

        c.   previous occupation

X   d.   adequacy of income

(E) 16. Since 1986, the mandatory retirement age for most occupations is:

        a.   62

        b.   65

        c.   70

X   d.   there is no mandatory retirement

(M) 17. Older people who are unemployed and seeking employment must overcome a number of common obstacles. Which of the following is/are frequently encountered?

        a.   subtle forms of age discrimination

        b.   employers' reluctance to retrain older workers

        c.   technological and workplace changes

        d.   "rusty" job-hunting techniques

X   e.   all of the above

(M) 18. A comprehensive approach to retirement planning should include:

        a.   financial planning

        b.   health promotion

        c.   leisure planning

        d.   restructuring of work patterns

X   e.   all of the above

(C)19. The primary reason for seeking employment after retirement is:

      a.   the desire to make a contribution to the community
      b.   the desire for the sociability of the job
X   c.   the need to supplement retirement income
      d.   boredom

(E)20. Which of the following statements is true regarding retirement?

      a.   Retirement has been found to be related to mental illness
      b.   Retirement has been found to cause an increase in the number of physical health problems experienced.
      c.   Most people retire because they have to (i.e. mandatory retirement).
      d.   Retirement has been found to be associated with a marked decrease in participation in community organizations.
X   e.   none of the above

(C) 21. Which of the following is true regarding Social Security?

      a.   It provides an adequate retirement income for most retirees.
      b.   Higher income workers benefit proportionately more than low-income workers.
X   c.   It is based upon the concept of earned rights (i.e., benefits in proportion to what a person has paid into the system).
      d.   all of the above.
      e.   none of the above

(E) 22. The largest source of income for older persons is:

      a.   savings and other assets
      b.   pensions
X   c.   Social Security
      d.   salary and wages

(M) 23. Job-specific private pensions:

      a.   cover all retirees of private companies
      b.   generally are equivalent to 80% of a retiree's employment income
      c.   typically include annual cost of living increases
X   d.   are more likely to benefit long-term, middle and upper-income employees.

(M) 24 Perceptions of older people as financially better off than any other age group overlook the fact that:
    a.   older people are more likely to be among the near-poor than other age groups
    b.   there are "hidden poor" among the older population
    c.   there are pockets of poverty among women, ethnic minorities, and the oldest-old

X   d.   all of the above
    e.   none of the above

(M) 25. The percentage of older people who fall below the official poverty line is:

    a.   approximately 50%
    b.   less than 5%
X   c.   approximately 10%
    d.   approximately 25%

(C) 26. Which of the following are characteristics of the Supplemental Security Income (SSI) program?
    a.   There are limits on assets and income.
    b.   Benefits can be reduced if relatives provide assistance.
    c.   More women than men depend on SSI.
    d.   The application process is complex.
X   e.   all of the above.

(E) 27. Among all age groups, the poorest are:

    a.   the young old, aged 60-65
    b.   all women under the age of 45
X   c.   ethnic minority women over age 75
    d.   ethnic minority men over age 75

(M) 28. If the Social Security program did not exist, the percentage of older people who would fall below the official poverty line would be:

    a.   about 75%
X   b.   about 55%
    c.   about 35%
    d.   about 15%

(C) 29. From the perspective of social phenomenologists, leisure is distinguished by:

      a.   free time
      b.   activity and "keeping busy"
X   c.   its intrinsic meaning
      d.   all of the above
      e.   none of the above

(M) 30. Leisure patterns in old age tend to:

X   a.   be marked by more solitary and sedentary activities compared to younger counterparts
      b.   show a departure from leisure activities in earlier years
      c.   have little association with feelings of well-being
      d.   consist of boring activities

(C) 31. Performing routine household chores can serve which of the following functions for an older person?
      a.   be a means to maintain competence levels in relation to changes
      b.   be a source of self-esteem
      c.   provide personal satisfaction
      d.   still be consistent with the concept of productive aging
X   e.   all of the above

(M) 32. Although senior centers can provide meaningful leisure activities, they do not serve the majority of older people. Reasons for this include:

      a.   poor health among many who would benefit
      b.   older people's prejudice against participating with other older adults
      c.   programs are often perceived as irrelevant to low-income older adults
      d.   few men participate
X   e.   all of the above

(M) 33. Voluntary association membership appears to be most strongly associated with life satisfaction when:
      a.   older people interact with younger people
X   b.   older people have significant and influential roles within the voluntary association
      c.   older people have numerous opportunities to socialize with younger people
      d.   older people have the money to join such associations

(E) 34. The social theory of aging which best explains patterns of volunteer activity in old age is:

a. disengagement
X b. continuity
c. person-environment
d. social exchange

(C) 35. Which of the following statements is false about older adults and volunteerism?

a. Older people who volunteer probably also volunteered when they were younger
X b. The retirement years are an ideal time to recruit older people as volunteers
c. Those older adults who volunteer generally derive personal satisfaction from these activities
d. Some aging advocates maintain that older volunteers should hold more responsible and/or paid positions
e. none of the above

(M) 36. Rates of volunteering are highest among older people who:

a. have higher income
b. are well educated
c. are married
d. are satisfied with their lives
X e. all of the above

(C) 37. Which of the following statements about religious participation is true?

a. Religious participation across the life span peaks in the late 60's or early 70's
b. Older people engage in fewer internal religious activities (such as reading the Bible) than other age groups
X c. Religious faith appears to be more influential in older people's lives than in other age groups
d. Individuals tend to become more religious as they age

(C) 38. Research on religiousness is limited by:

X a. cross-sectional data
b. longitudinal data
c. no attention to gender and ethnic minority status
d. all of the above
e. none of the above

(M) 39. Religious involvement can be an effective coping mechanism and source of social support, particularly for:
    a.   those over age 85
X   b.   ethnic minority elders
    c.   Caucasian women
    d.   none of the above

(C) 40. Which of the following statements about political participation is false?

    a.   In general, older people today vote more conservatively than younger people, though this varies by issue.
X   b.   Rates of voting decline sharply with an increase in age
    c.   When variables such as education are controlled for, interest in politics increases with age
    d.   On some issues, older people vote more liberally than younger people
    e.   none of the above

(C) 41. When looking at the political behavior of older people, it is necessary to:

X   a.   take account of the historical period in which they were raised
    b.   compare the behavior of individuals of various ages at one point in time
    c.   take account of their age
    d.   try to isolate age differences

(M) 42. Instances of low voter turnout among the older population can generally be explained in terms of:
    a.   mistrust of the political process
    b.   gender
    c.   education
X   d.   all of the above
    e.   none of the above

(M) 43. Spiritual well-being can generally be characterized by:

    a.   achieving a sense of purpose or meaning for one's continued existence
    b.   high rates of participation in organized religion
    c.   mental well-being
    d.   all of the above
X   e.   a and c

(M) 44. Health care providers are beginning to pay attention to the spiritual dimensions of health care because of:

    a.   the interrelationship between spiritual well-being and good health
    b.   the role of spirituality in health promotion
    c.   the importance of spirituality in dealing with loss
X   d.   all of the above
    e.   none of the above

(C) 45. The argument that older people as a group are politically powerful is based on the assumption that:

    a.   older adults have a relatively high ratio of voting and political party membership
    b.   there is a growing shared political consciousness among older people
    c.   there will be better health and higher education among future older cohorts
X   d.   all of the above
    e.   none of the above

(C) 46. Which of the following statements is advanced by critics about the perspective that older adults are unified and are a significant political force?

    a.   The heterogeneity of the older population precludes their sharing an age-based consciousness
    b.   Increasingly, older and younger people are forming cross-age alliances
    c.   Senior organizations have not had a substantial and long-term impact on social policy, especially for the most disadvantaged groups
    d.   Past legislative success has resulted primarily from politicians' beliefs that older adults are worse off and more deserving than other age groups
X   e.   all of the above

(E) 47. The largest and most influential senior organization is:

    a.   National Council of Senior Citizens
    b.   Gerontological Society of America
X   c.   American Association of Retired Persons
    d.   National Council on the Aging

True or False

(E) 1. Most people experience retirement as a time of dramatic changes in their leisure activities and interests.
   True ___   False X

(M) 2. Deterioration in mental or physical health is a primary consequence of retirement.
   True ___   False X

(M) 3. Mandatory retirement is no longer the major reason for early retirement.
   True X   False ___

(C) 4. Employment studies show that older workers are as productive as younger workers but their absenteeism rate is higher.
   True ___   False X

(M) 5. Once out of work, workers over age 40 remain unemployed longer and are more likely to become discouraged than younger persons.
   True X   False ___

(M) 6. Most major employers are restructuring the workplace to encourage older adults to work longer.
   True ___   False X

(C) 7. In recent years, employee pension coverage and benefits are increasing.
   True ___   False X

(M) 8. Marital satisfaction generally increases because of retirement.
   True ___   False X

(E) 9. The age at which workers can collect full Social Security benefits is 65 years.
   True X   False ___

(E) 10. The primary source of income in retirement is personal savings.
   True ___   False X

(M) 11. Older women are more likely to work part-time than their male counterparts.
   True X   False ___

(C) 12. Nowadays, there are increasingly clear and sharp distinctions between the status of worker and that of retiree.
   True ___   False X

(M) 13. Changes in the workplace in the 1990's have tended to benefit the older workers.

True ___   False X

(C) 14. Social Security provisions favor the two-career family.

True ___   False X

(M) 15. Homemakers are automatically covered by Social Security based on their own contribution to the home.

True ___   False X

(C) 16. Fortunately, the majority of older people have benefits from both pensions and Social Security.

True ___   False X

(M) 17. The proportion of men and women over age 65 who are employed in the 1990s is smaller than ever before.

True X   False ___

(E) 18. The poverty rate among the older population has decreased since the late 1960s, largely because of benefits from Social Security and Medicare.

True X   False ___

(M) 19. Eligibility for Supplemental Security Income (SSI) is determined on the basis of number of years worked in covered employment.

True ___   False X

(C) 20. A primary reason for some older adults' low socioeconomic status is that Social Security has not kept pace with inflation.

True ___   False X

(M) 21. In order to derive satisfaction from life, older people must be involved in active leisure pursuits.

True ___   False X

(C) 22. The quality of interactions in leisure pursuits tends to be related to higher life satisfaction and morale than the number and type of leisure pursuits.

True X   False ___

(M) 23. The most important factor in determining membership in voluntary associations is age.

True ___   False X

(M) 24. Rates of volunteering do not change much after retirement.

True X   False ___

(M) 25. People typically become more religious as they grow older.
True ___   False _X_

(E) 26. Religious activities and attitudes have generally been found to be associated with life satisfaction and adjustment to old age.
True _X_   False ___

(E) 27. Spirituality has been found to have little relation to life satisfaction and quality of life.
True ___   False _X_

(C) 28. Older people are more likely to vote in national elections than are younger voters.
True _X_   False ___

(C) 29. As people age, they generally become more conservative in their voting patterns.
True ___   False _X_

(M) 30. Age is the primary factor in determining how individuals vote on different issues, such as health care and abortion rights.
True ___   False _X_

(E) 31. Most activities by national senior organizations have not addressed the needs of low-income older individuals.
True _X_   False ___

(E) 32. Educational institutions have taken the lead in developing programs specifically for older adults.
True ___   False _X_

(E) 33. Church attendance is not a good indicator of religiosity among older people.
True _X_   False ___

CHAPTER 12: DEATH, DYING, BEREAVEMENT, AND WIDOWHOOD

Glossary

Advance Directive
Anticipatory Grief
Appropriate Death
Bereavement
Bereavement Overload
Choices in Dying
Compassion in Dying
Conservator
Death Crisis
Death System
Death with Dignity
Durable Power of Attorney
Dying Process
Euthanasia

Grief Process
Guardian
Hemlock Society
Hospice
Living Dying Interval
Living Will
Mourning
Natural Death Acts
Palliative Treatment
Patient Self-Determination Act
Passive Euthanasia
Right to Die
Dying Trajectory

Topics for Discussion

1.   What are ways in which our society seeks to deny or avoid death? How do these influence your own attitudes toward death?

2.   What are some limitations of Kubler-Ross's stage model of dying? Does this model "fit" with your experience when someone is dying? Are you aware of other models about death and dying that address some of these limitations?

3.   Discuss ways that psycho-social factors interact with the biological process of dying.

4.   What are some issues for people to consider when preparing for death? What can you do in your own life to prepare for your own death?

5.   What is your own position on euthanasia? With regard to older people? With regard to youth? What would you want for yourself if you were terminally ill? What would you include if you were writing a Living Will?

6.   What can human service professionals do to protect the rights of dying patients and to ensure a "good death"? Discuss ways that these goals may be in conflict with one another.

7.   Given increased life expectancy and life-prolonging medical techniques, discuss both the ethical and legal issues related to dying..

8.   If you were a health care professional working in a nursing home, what kinds of services would you develop to help older residents and their relatives cope with dying, death and bereavement?

Multiple Choice

(C) 1. Cultures develop different views on dying. Which of the following perspectives is true of our society?
   a. Death is viewed as an unnatural event which is to be fought off
   b. Death is viewed primarily as a province of the old.
   c. Death is both denied and accepted.
   d. Some types of rituals such as funerals can ease the mourning process.
X e. all of the above

(E) 2. Before the twentieth century, death:

X a. generally occurred at home
   b. was a phenomenon largely of old age
   c. was peripheral to younger people's awareness
   d. all of the above

(C) 3. Studies of fears of death indicate that:

   a. older adults are morbidly fearful of death
   b. fear of death increases among those with terminal conditions
X c. older people typically have fewer fears about death than younger people do
   d. most older adults do not think about death very much
   e. none of the above

(C) 4. Older adults may fear death less than younger people because:

   a. older adults view their lives as having less future promise and less value
   b. older adults often have a sense of living on "borrowed time"
   c. older adults' experiences with the deaths of relatives and friends can help them anticipate and accept dying
   d. dying later in life is an "on-time" event
X e. all of the above.

(M) 5. Which of the following is not a stage in the dying process, as presented by Kubler-Ross?
   a. denial
   b. anger
X c. hope
   d. bargaining

(E) 6.　In Kubler-Ross' stages of dying, patients typically:

        a.　go through the stages in exact order
        b.　finally make it to acceptance
X   c.　may move back and forth between stages, and be in several stages at once
        d.　do not usually deny their diagnosis

(M) 7.　The dying trajectory framework recognizes that:

X   a.　the dying patient, family members, and helping professionals all perceive a course of dying and an expected time of death.
        b.　there is no predictability to the pace of dying.
        c.　professionals, family members, and the dying person nearly always agree about the pace of dying.
        d.　none of the above

(C) 8.　Which of the following are common criticisms of Kubler-Ross' theory?

        a.　Dying individuals often go through stages in different sequence and may repeat some.
        b.　For some people, denial or anger may be a healthier way to face death than acceptance is.
        c.　Dying people tend to experience a variety of reactions rather than an orderly progression of stages.
X   d.　all of the above
        e.　none of the above

(M) 9.　Hospice care includes:

        a.　a philosophy of care for the terminally ill
        b.　support for families of dying persons
        c.　methods to minimize the pain experienced by the terminally ill
X   d.　all of the above
        e.　none of the above

(E) 10.　Increased recognition of the needs of dying patients has led to the development of:

        a.　legal and medical debates about the right to die
        b.　hospices
        c.　counseling programs for the dying and their families
X   d.　all of the above
        e.　none of the above

(E) 11. The primary emphasis of hospice is:

      a.   extending life
      b.   curing disease
X   c.   quality of life
      d.   diagnosing disease

(C) 12. Proponents of the right to die with dignity would disagree with which of the following statements?

X   a.   Most older people should die in a hospital to ensure the best care.
      b.   Doctors know more about treating illness than about palliative care.
      c.   The high cost of dying is burdening the health care system.
      d.   Helping an older person obtain a good death is a desirable goal.

(M) 13. The general public's attitude toward the "right to die" is that:

      a.   it is immoral.
      b.   active euthanasia is best.
X   c.   people of all ages should have the right to refuse treatment.
      d.   only older adults should have the right to refuse treatment.

(M) 14. Suspending all available treatment, including feeding or a ventilator, in order to relieve suffering is called:

X   a.   passive euthanasia
      b.   active euthanasia
      c.   mercy killing
      d.   all of the above

(M) 15. Taking actions deliberately to shorten a person's life, such as providing a lethal injection, in order to end suffering is called:
      a.   passive euthanasia
      b.   voluntary elective death
X   c.   active euthanasia
      d.   failure to care

(M) 16. The study of issues such as euthanasia is called:

      a.   psychoethics
      b.   socioethics
X   c.   bioethics
      d.   medethics

(C) 17. Assisted suicide is characterized by:

     a.   another person provides the means by which an individual ends his or her life
     b.   it is legal in only one state
     c.   it is supported by the Hemlock Society
     d.   public support for it is growing
X   e.   all of the above

(E) 18. A Living Will is a document that states:

     a.   the terms of the writer's estate
     b.   the writer's religious belief
X   c.   what medical action, if any, should be taken if the writer becomes mentally incompetent or terminally ill
     d.   all of the above
     e.   none of the above

(C) 19. A Durable Power of Attorney:

     a.   applies only to the terminally ill
     b.   is a substitute for a living will
X   c.   appoints another person to make decisions in the event the writer becomes incompetent
     d.   all of the above

(C) 20. A legal document that establishes control over an individual's person, property and finances is called a:
     a.   conservatorship
     b.   Living Will
X   c.   guardianship
     d.   durable power of attorney

(E) 21. Don's wife is terminally ill, and he has begun to grieve. This is called _____ grief.

     a.   preparatory
     b.   premature
     c.   inappropriate
X   d.   anticipatory

(M) 22. Which of the following stages do not typically occur in the grief reaction to death?

     a.   shock, numbness, and disbelief
     b.   idealization of the loved one who has died
     c.   reorganization
X   d.   hope

(M) 23. The way in which we express our grief, which is culturally influenced, is called:

         a.   grief work
X   b.   mourning
         c.   bereavement
         d.   working through

(M) 24. In working with relatives regarding their grief, health care providers must:

X   a.   be sensitive to cultural and ethnic differences regarding death
         b.   discourage relatives from spending money on a funeral
         c.   help move them quickly to the acceptance phase of grief
         d.   all of the above

(E) 25. Older widows may find widowhood to be more difficult than older widowers do because the former:

X   a.   are more likely to face financial hardships
         b.   have fewer friends to turn to
         c.   move in with adult children shortly after their spouse's death
         d.   have more difficulty expressing their grief

(M) 26. Women become widows at the average age of:
         a.   72
         b.   60
X   c.   66
         d.   56

(E) 27. Women who cope best with widowhood seem to be those who:

         a.   see their children frequently
X   b.   have a network of friends
         c.   were widowed early in life
         d.   all of the above

(C) 28. The death of a spouse may be one of the most stressful events that an older person will experience because:

        a.   typically, it negatively affects the surviving spouse's health.
        b.   for most people, it leads to long-term difficulties in coping.
        c.   depression, loneliness and sadness become chronic e.g. ongoing).
        d.   all of the above

X   e.   none of the above

(C) 29. One mistake that people frequently make with their bereaved loved ones is:

        a.   to allow people to grieve in their own way
        b.   to allow people to grieve for as long as they desire

X   c.   to underestimate the amount of time needed for grieving
        d.   to encourage the bereaved to attend an appropriate support group

TRUE OR FALSE

(E) 1. One of the major assumptions of Kubler-Ross's work is that dying can be a time of growth and meaning.
      True _X_   False ___

(E) 2. Kubler-Ross' stages of dying appear to be universal.
      True _X_   False ___

(E) 3. Psychotherapy is of limited personal value to older dying patients.
      True ___   False _X_

(M) 4. Most states have legislation that permits relatives to actively aid a dying person in ending their life.
      True ___   False _X_

(E) 5. An example of passive euthanasia is deliberately giving a lethal injection to end a patient's suffering.
      True ___   False _X_

(C) 6. Passive euthanasia is constitutionally protected.
      True _X_   False ___

(C) 7. Withholding or withdrawing useless or unwanted medical treatments for patients close to death is both illegal and unethical.
      True ___   False _X_

.(M) 8. Public and professional acceptance of euthanasia is decreasing.
      True ___   False _X_

(M) 9. Younger widows generally find the death of a husband to be more stressful than older widows do, especially in the early stages of grief.
      True _X_   False ___

(M) 10. Grief is always less when death is not sudden and the survivors have been able to anticipate it and prepare for changes.
      True ___   False _X_

(E) 11. The major problem faced by both widowers and widows is loneliness.
      True _X_   False ___

(E) 12. Widow support groups recognize the value of informal help from people who have had similar experiences.
      True _X_   False ___

(M) 13. About half of American women become widows around age 66.
         True _X_   False ___

(E) 14. Women are more likely than men to remarry after the death of a spouse.
         True ___   False _X_

(E) 15. Most survivors successfully resolve their grief within a year.
         True ___   False _X_

CHAPTER 13: THE RESILIENCY OF OLDER ETHNIC MINORITIES

Glossary

Acculturation

Antimiscegenation

Double Jeopardy Hypothesis

Epidemiology

Ethnogerontology

Fictive Kin

Homogeneity

Indian Health Service

Law of Primogeniture

Life Course Perspective

Topics for Discussion

1. What are the major problems facing ethnic minority elders in our society? What do you perceive to be some solutions to these problems? Barriers to these solutions? What do you perceive to be strengths of ethnic minority elders?

2. Apply social exchange theory to an analysis of the status of ethnic minority elders in our society. Cite examples that illustrate the centrality of control over valued resources to their status.

3. Older persons are not a homogeneous population. Identify dimensions along which ethnic minority elders differ from and are similar to the older population in general. Drawing upon your own discipline's research and practice perspective, what are some implications of these dimensions for both research and the delivery of services?

4. Suggest directions for future research on ethnic minority elders. What are some of the difficulties of conducting such research?

5. Describe your own ethnic and cultural experiences and how those might affect your own aging process and that of other members of your family.

6. If you were designing a multicultural senior center, describe typical programs and how they would differ from more traditional centers and from programs for a specific ethnic group.

7. Describe your own perceptions of the older population of a specific ethnic minority group. To what extent are these stereotypes? To what extent are these based on personal experiences? Do you have any research support for your perceptions?

Multiple Choice

(M) 1. Which of the following characteristics is generally associated with ethnic minority status?
    a. lifetime experience with discrimination
    b. unique historical and cultural events
    c. development of coping structures and support systems
X   d. all of the above

(C) 2. The double jeopardy hypothesis, as first advanced by Tally and Kaplan, suggests that:
    a. with age, differences in income, health and life expectancy diminish.
    b. women face more disadvantages than men as they age.
X   c. lifetime factors of economic and racial discrimination make it more difficult for ethnic minorities to adjust to old age than for whites.
    d. none of the above

(M) 3. All ethnic minority populations share the following characteristic:

    a. The young outnumber the old.
    b. Their median age is lower than for the white population.
    c. They face more economic and health problems than the white population does.
X   d. all of the above.

(E) 4. Compared with the American older population generally, elders in minority groups are:
    a. less likely to have access to adequate health care
    b. more likely to have chronic illnesses
    c. more likely to be poor
    d. less likely to be in a nursing home
X   e. all of the above.

(E) 5. The poverty of most ethnic minority elders tends to reflect which of the following conditions?
    a. lifelong patterns of unemployment and underemployment
    b. employment in jobs not covered by Social Security
    c. employment in jobs not covered by private pensions
    d. intermittent employment (i.e., movement in and out of the labor market)
X   e. all of the above.

(C) 6. The ethnic minority population that forms the smallest percentage of the total population age 65 and over is:
- a. African Americans
- b. Asian Americans / Pacific Islanders

X c. American Indians
- d. Hispanic Americans

(C) 7. Which of the following statements describing the African American elders is true?

- a. They have a lower prevalence of chronic diseases than whites.
- b. There are proportionately more African American elders in nursing homes compared to whites.
- c. They receive a greater percentage of Social Security benefits than whites.

X d. After age 85, they become "better survivors."

(C) 8. Which of the following statements describing African American elders is false?

- a. They are poorer than whites.
- b. They are not as healthy as whites.

X c. Their life expectancy at birth is as long as whites.
- d. They are less well educated than whites.

(M) 9. The African American extended family is generally characterized by:

- a. older female family members frequently caring for young children
- b. shared living arrangements because of economic necessity
- c. adult children frequently providing care for older family members

X d. all of the above
- e. none of the above

(M)10. A major source of social and emotional support for African Americans, outside of family, is:
- a. the federal government
- b. senior centers

X c. the church
- d. self-help groups
- e. none of the above

(C) 11. Compared to their white counterparts, the proportion of African American men to women is higher among the:

- a. baby boomers
- b. young-old
- c. old-old

X d. oldest-old

106

(C) 12. Differences between whites and African Americans in life expectancy at age 65 are:

        a.   greater than differences in life expectancy at birth

X   b.   less than differences in life expectancy at birth

        c.   about the same as life expectancy at birth

        d.   due to higher infant mortality among whites

(M) 13. Which of the following statements regarding Hispanic American elders is true?

        a.   The majority live in rural areas.

X   b.   They are composed of several different subgroups, each with a distinct national/cultural heritage.

        c.   They use health services proportionately more than whites and other ethnic minorities.

        d.   Their median age is significantly higher than whites and other ethnic minorities.

(M) 14. A major reason that some Hispanics do not seek out social services is:

        a.   their relatives provide all the assistance they need.

X   b.   they may have been illegal immigrants and fear deportation

        c.   they do not want assistance.

        d.   they expect the service system to seek them out.

(C) 15. Among Hispanic families, older members have traditionally:

        a.   played only a minor role in child-rearing

        b.   been ignored by younger members

X   c.   received a great deal of respect and community support compared to their Anglo counterparts

        d.   had little influence in family decision-making

(C) 16. Which of the following statements about American Indian elders is true?

        a.   The Bureau of Indian Affairs has supported the traditional roles of American Indian elders.

X   b.   Diseases such as TB, cirrhosis of the liver, and diabetes are common.

        c.   They are frequent users of public social and health services.

        d.   A small percentage live with other family members.

(M) 17. Asian American / Pacific Islander elders have long been underserved by mainstream social and health services because:

         a.   they have so few problems

X   b.   they face language barriers and are often socially isolated

         c.   they are primarily women

         d.   they are financially better off than other ethnic minority groups

(C) 18. Asian American elders differ from other ethnic minority groups in that:

         a.   they are primarily third generation

         b.   there are proportionately more women than in other ethnic groups

X   c.   there are proportionately more men than in other ethnic groups

         d.   they underutilize social and health services

(C) 19. Which of the following statements about Asian American elders is <u>false</u>?

         a.   Those who immigrated to the U.S. before 1924 are less educated, less likely to speak English, and more economically disadvantaged.

X   b.   They are high utilizers of medical services and hospital care.

         c.   More live below the poverty line than their white counterparts.

         d.   They often fail to apply for public assistance programs for which they are qualified.

(M) 20. The least amount of data is available about the status of:

         a.   African American elders

         b.   Hispanic American elders

X   c.   American Indian elders

         d.   Asian American elders

(E) 21. Which of the following factors would not serve to increase the utilization of social and health services by older ethnic minorities?

         a.   increased numbers of bilingual staff

         b.   services that build upon and respect cultural values and community strengths

X   c.   centralized services for all ethnic minorities to use

         d.   free transportation provided to services

(E) 22. In developing health and long-term care for ethnic minority elders, it is important to:

       a.   be sensitive to the utilization of folk medicine and healing
       b.   formulate an holistic and wellness-oriented approach
       c.   utilize the informal supports of family, friends and community
X   d.   all of the above
       e.   none of the above

(M) 23. Low rates of nursing home placement among ethnic minority populations are due to which of the following factors:

       a.   inadequate income to be able to pay for private nursing homes
       b.   reliance on informal supports and traditional folk medicine
       c.   current or historical racist practices among medical providers and nursing home staff
X   d.   all of the above
       e.   none of the above

True or False

(M) 1. Ethnicity refers to minority status within our society.
    True ___   False _X_

(M) 2. For all ethnic minority populations, a proportionately smaller percentage of older members are in nursing homes than among white elders.
    True _X_   False ___

(C) 3. The racial minority crossover phenomenon refers to findings that the death rate for African Americans age 85 and over is lower than for whites age 85 and over.
    True _X_   False ___

(M) 4. African American elders tend to be highly dissatisfied with their lives.
    True ___   False _X_

(M) 5. The primary factor underlying the relative youthfulness of the Hispanic American population is its high mortality rate.
    True ___   False _X_

(E) 6. Compared to other groups of older adults, American Indian elders tend to turn more to governmental programs for support.
    True ___   False _X_

(M) 7. Chronological age is probably the worst way to identify the need for services among older American Indians.
    True _X_   False ___

(E) 8. Compared to their white counterparts, Asian American / Pacific Islander elders are more likely to live in extended family arrangements.
    True _X_   False ___

(E) 9. The primary factor underlying the low utilization of social and health services by all ethnic minority groups is strong family support systems which can take care of their older relatives.
    True ___   False _X_

(C) 10. There is much disagreement among service providers about the need for preferential services targeted to ethnic minorities.
    True _X_   False ___

(M) 11. Barriers to service utilization can be conceptualized as primarily due to cultural factors.

True ___   False _X_

(M) 12. Today, life expectancy among older minorities is lower than for whites.

True _X_   False ___

(M) 13. The proportion of people aged 65 and older among ethnic minority groups will increase more than among whites in the 21st century

True _X_   False ___

CHAPTER 14: THE CHALLENGES FACING OLDER WOMEN

Glossary

Displaced homemakers
Estrogen
Hormone Replacement Therapy
Hot Flashes
Mammography
Menopause

Older Women's League
Osteoporosis
Postmenopause
Progesterone

Topics for Discussion

1.   Compare the status of men and women in old age. What are some of the reasons for gender-related differences in old age?

2.   How can you explain the fact that women live longer than men but are less healthy than their male counterparts in old age?

3.   In designing policies and programs for older women, what are factors about their socialization experiences that you would need to consider? How would you try to address these?

4.   What do you view to be the major problems facing older women in our culture? From the perspective of your discipline, what are two strategies toward solving the problems facing older women?

5.   What do you perceive to be the major strengths/resources of older women? From a policy or program perspective, what would be strategies for building upon these strengths?

6.   What types of policy changes are needed to address the economic problems faced by older women?

Multiple Choice

(E) 1. The primary reason that older women have become a special focus of some gerontological research is:

      a.   they form the fastest growing segment of our population.
      b.   they are more likely to face social problems than older men are.
      c.   they live longer than men.
X   d.   all of the above

(M) 2. From a feminist perspective, many of the problems faced by older women can be understood as:

      a.   the result of individual differences
      b.   an outcome of their socialization
X   c.   due to gender-based differences in power and privilege
      d.   all of the above
      e.   none of the above

(E) 3. The greatest problem faced by older women today is:

      a.   osteoporosis
      b.   menopause
X   c.   inadequate income
      d.   mental illness

(M) 4. The percentage of older women living in poverty is:

      a.   over 70%
      b.   less than 10%
X   c.   approximately 16%
      d.   approximately 33%

(M) 5. Among older women, the risk of poverty is associated with:

      a.   ethnic minority status
      b.   living alone
      c.   increased age
      d.   none of the above
X   e.   all of the above

(C) 6. There is a saying that "women are only one man away from poverty", and therefore at higher risk than their male counterparts. Why would that be true?

    a.   Homemakers are not eligible for Social Security based on their status.
    b.   If a women is employed, she is often paid less than a man in the same position.
    c.   If a women is employed, she is often in a field that pays less than fields that men typically enter.
    d.   none of the above

X   e.   all of the above

(C) 7. The issue of caregiving provides an opportunity for feminist researchers to:

    a.   control for the effects of gender
X   b.   recognize the interconnections between women's paid and unpaid work
    c.   identify only gender variations
    d.   none of the above
    e.   all of the above

(E) 8. Women's retirement income is generally characterized by which of the following?

    a.   They usually collect full Social Security benefits.
    b.   They generally collect Social Security benefits on the basis of their own employment history.
X   c.   They are more likely than their male counterparts to collect only the minimum Social Security benefits.
    d.   They typically enjoy the combined income of Social Security and private pensions.

(C) 9. Social Security affects older women in which of the following ways?

    a.   Women's benefits tend to be lower than men's.
    b.   Widows with survivors' benefits generally receive lower benefits than retired workers do.
    c.   Women who are divorced before ten years of marriage are not entitled to any of their former husband's benefits.
    d.   A homemaker receives no Social Security credit for her work.
X   e.   none of the above

(C) 10. Older women's participation in private pension systems has been characterized by the fact that:

       a.   most women get by financially on survivors' benefits selected by their husbands.

X   b.   pension systems reward the long-term steady worker with high earnings and job stability.

       c.   divorced women can still enjoy their former husbands' pension benefit.

       d.   pension provisions enacted by Congress in 1980 will fortunately benefit this current cohort of retired women.

(E) 11. Older women's lower economic status than men's is due to which of the following factors:

       a.   their greater likelihood of being family caregivers at all stages of life

       b.   their concentration in lower-paying jobs without benefits

       c.   their lower probability of receiving a private pension

X   d.   all of the above

       e.   none of the above

(M) 12. Compared to their male counterparts, older women's health status is characterized as follows:

       a.   they are healthier.

X   b.   they are more likely to face non-fatal chronic conditions.

       c.   they experience fewer days of restricted activity and disability.

       d.   they are less likely to take curative action when they are ill.

(C) 13. The major reason that older women have less access to group health insurance of their own is:

       a.   women are not as healthy as men.

       b.   women visit doctors more often than men.

X   c.   women are less likely to be employed or are only sporadically employed compared to men.

       d.   women can rely upon their husbands' insurance.

       e.   women can depend on Medicare to cover their health care costs.

(E) 14. A primary reason that women age 75 and over are more likely to be institutionalized than older men is:

       a.   they are not as healthy as their male counterparts age 75 and over.

       b.   they are less likely to be married.

       c.   they have fewer available resources for home-based care.

       d.   they are likely to have outlived some of their children.

X   e.   all of the above

(M) 15. Which of the following statements is false when describing the social status of older women?

      a.   They have fewer chances to remarry than their male counterparts.

X   b.   They have fewer close friends than older men.

      c.   They are more likely to be widowed than older men.

      d.   Those living alone are in greater need of social and health services.

      e.   They are more likely to rely on adult children for support than on their husbands.

(E) 16. Among all age groups, the poorest are:

      a.   the young old, aged 60-65

      b.   all women under the age of 45

X   c.   ethnic minority women over age 75

      d.   ethnic minority men over age 75

      e.   none of the above

True or False

(E) 1. Because they comprise the majority of the older population, old women have long been the focus of gerontological research.

     True ___   False <u>X</u>

(E) 2. A primary reason for older women's economic vulnerability is that most women did not work consistently for pay throughout their lives.

     True <u>X</u>   False ___

(E) 3. Osteoporosis is especially problematic because of the associated risk of bone fractures.

     True <u>X</u>   False ___

(E) 4. The majority of older women live with their husbands or other family members.

     True ___   False <u>X</u>

(C) 5. Eighty-five percent of women outlive their husbands.

     True <u>X</u>   False ___

(E) 6. Compared to men, women have more social resources to draw upon in old age.

     True <u>X</u>   False ___

(M) 7. The Older Women's League is a political interest group open only to women age 65 and over.

     True ___   False <u>X</u>

(M) 8. Fortunately, the economic status of old women in the future will be substantially improved over the current cohort.

     True ___   False <u>X</u>

CHAPTER 15: SOCIAL POLICIES TO ADDRESS SOCIAL PROBLEMS

Glossary

Cost Containment

Cost Effectiveness

Cost Efficiency

Cost of Living Adjustments (COLA)

Dependency Ration

Direct Benefit

Eligibility Criteria

Entitlement Programs

Generation X

Generational Investment

Income Redistribution

Incremental

Index

Indirect Benefit

Individual Equity

Information and Referral

Intergenerational Inequity

Means or Need Based Entitlements

Non-contributory Programs

Outreach

Payroll Taxes

Policy

Politics of Entitlement

Politics of Productivity

Residual Role of Government

Respite Care

Selective Benefits

Social Adequacy

Social Insurance

Social Programs

Universal Benefits

Topics for Discussion

1.   What factors underlie the relatively slow development of social policy for older adults in the United States, and the incremental, residual nature of the policies that have been formulated? How does this contrast with other Western industrialized societies?

2.   Identify the pros and cons of age-based verses needs-based services. Which approach -- or combination of approaches -- do you support and why?

3.   What do you perceive to be some limitations/gaps of the current Social Security system? What is your position on the advantages and disadvantages of recommendations to privatize Social Security, such as encouraging enrollees to invest part of their payroll taxes in the stock market?

4.   Debate the arguments expressed by the intergenerational inequity proponents and those of the interdependence of generations perspective. What are the strengths and limitations of each argument? Where do you stand in terms of these arguments? What is the evidence to support your position? In your discussion, address the strengths of the "politics of productivity" and the "New Aging" paradigm.

5.   What is your perspective on the appropriate division of responsibility between the public and private sectors in addressing problems facing older people? Provide a rationale for your point of view.

6.   What are the primary ways that the social policies of the "New Aging" in the post-1990's will differ from current public policies?

7.   Identify one major societal change that you view as necessary to improve the quality of older persons' lives. What are the barriers to this change? What would be a strategy to bring about the needed change?

Multiple Choice

(M) 1. Programs for the older population have been slow to develop in the U.S. because:

        a.   our current older population is so small.

        b.   families have traditionally cared for their older relatives.

X   c.   our culture places a high value on independence and self-reliance.

        d.   our older population has not needed assistance until recently.

(M) 2. The development of policies for older adults has benefited from:

        a.   our cultural value on individual responsibility

X   b.   public perceptions of older people as more deserving than other age groups

        c.   the fiscal conservatism of the 1980's

        d.   the government's long-range planning capabilities

(M) 3. Estes' critique of the manner in which social policies for older adults have developed in our society is that:

        a.   human service professionals have benefited more than low-income elders.

        b.   older people are defined as a social problem rather than looking at underlying structural causes of problems.

        c.   the solution to the problems faced by older people tends to be to provide medical services.

        d.   older people are perceived as different from other age groups, therefore requiring separate services

X   e.   all of the above

(C) 4. Most policies that benefit the older population are:

        a.   categorical (age-based) and means-tested

X   b.   categorical and universal for all older people

        c.   direct cash transfers on the basis of mean-tests

        d.   noncontributory and categorical

(M) 5. The Social Security System is characterized by:

        a.   universal eligibility for all persons

        b.   ensuring sufficient retirement income

X   c.   providing a minimum floor of protection for those who have earned it

        d.   all of the above

(M) 6. New proposals to privatize Social Security are characterized by:

       a.   increased government regulation
       b.   expectations that the government will more effectively invest Social Security funds
X   c.   a shift away from the basic philosophy of social insurance
       d.   all of the above
       e.   none of the above

(M) 7. Private pensions can be described as:

       a.   available to nearly 90% of retirees
X   b.   intensifying economic inequalities among the older population
       c.   providing an adequate floor of protection to pension recipients
       d.   available in most of the growing number of positions in the service sector

(C) 8. Which of the following factors affects the revenues available in the Social Security trust fund?

       a.   levels of unemployment
       b.   changes in the age of eligibility for Social Security benefits
       c.   the changing dependency ratios
X   d.   all of the above
       e.   none of the above

(C) 9. A major negative consequence of Title XX (Social Services Block Grant) funding is that:

X   a.   low income elders generally compete with other poor groups for resources.
       b.   it provides for only financial support, not other types of assistance.
       c.   income is the only criterion for eligibility.
       d.   dependent children are excluded from funding.

(M) 10. The agency responsible for administering the programs and services of the Older Americans Act is:
       a.   the Social Security Division
X   b.   the Administration on Aging
       c.   the Federal Council on Aging
       d.   the Leadership Council on Aging

(E) 11. The primary source of funds of social services specifically for older people is:

      a.   Medicare and Medicaid
      b.   Social Security
      c.   Supplemental Security Income
X   d.   the Older Americans Act and Title XX

(C) 12. The perspective that services should be determined on the basis of need, not age, maintains that:

      a.   age is an arbitrary criterion for service delivery.
      b.   age-based criteria stigmatize the older adult.
      c.   age-based criteria assume that older people are different from other age groups.
      d.   old age alone is not sufficient grounds for public benefits
X   e.   all of the above

(M) 13. Which of the following viewpoints is not advanced by supporters of the intergenerational inequity perspective?
      a.   Younger people will not receive fair returns for their Social Security investments.
X   b.   Older and younger people have both been hard hit by inflation
      c.   Older adults are draining the federal budget.
      d.   Children are poorer than older people are.

(C) 14. A basic assumption of the interdependence of generations framework is that:

      a.   older adults are financially better off than other age groups.
X   b.   the family is a major mechanism for intergenerational transfers.
      c.   the younger generation only benefits from Social Security when they live long enough to retire.
      d.   our society needs to achieve equity or fairness between generations.

(C)15. Since the late 1980's, policy development for the older population has been affected by:

      a.   perceptions of the older population as "greedy geezers"
      b.   the growing federal deficit
      c.   the increasing socioeconomic diversity of the older population
      d.   reductions in funding for federal programs
X   e.   all of the above

(M) 16. The "politics of productivity" differ from the "politics of entitlement" in the following ways:

    a. resources are provided on the basis of age.
    b. older adults are viewed as more worthy than other age groups.
X   c. older adults are viewed as a resource, providing intergenerational assistance.
    d. all of the above
    e. none of the above

(C) 17. Which of the following does not characterize the politics of the "New Aging"?

    a. an intergenerational perspective
    b. the diversity of the older population
X   c. an age-based perspective on services
    d. a concern for future generations
    e. none of the above

(C) 18. The following trend is of concern to many policy makers and citizens groups, such as the Concord Coalition and the Third Millennium:
    a. the growth of entitlement programs
    b. the rapid growth of programs that benefit primarily older people
    c. the prediction that Social Security trust funds will be exhausted by 2029
    d. the perception that the older population is benefiting at the expense of younger people
X   e. all of the above

(M) 19. Citizen advocacy groups that are organized to advance public policy in the late 1990s and into the 21st century are likely to be characterized by:
    a. cultural homogeneity
    b. age homogeneity
X   c. alliances that cross cut age, gender, socioeconomic status and ethnic minority status
    d. political homogeneity
    e. none of the above

(M) 20. All of the following are fundamental to the Social Security system except for:

    a. the concept of social insurance
X   b, means-testing
    c. universal eligibility
    d. entitlement

True or False

(M) 1. The time period in which most of the policies and programs for older people were developed was during the 1980's.

True ___ False <u>X</u>

(C) 2. The growing federal and state allocations to programs for older adults have served to create a comprehensive and coordinated system of services.

True ___ False <u>X</u>

(E) 3. Social policies for older people tend to be residual and incremental in nature.

True <u>X</u> False ___

(M) 4. The "compassionate" stereotype of older adults as more deserving than other age groups strongly influences current policy developments.

True ___ False <u>X</u>

(M) 5. Eligibility for most policies and programs for older people is determined on the basis of age

True <u>X</u> False ___

(C) 6. Social Security and Medicare per se have been the primary causes of the growing federal deficit.

True ___ False <u>X</u>

(C) 7. The primary cause of the Social Security crisis in the early 1980's was the rapid growth of the older population.

True ___ False <u>X</u>

(M) 8. Tax benefits are an example of a policy that serves to benefit nearly all older people.

True ___ False <u>X</u>

(M) 9. The majority of the US population supports the current Social Security system.

True <u>X</u> False ___

(M) 10. The politics of the "New Aging" includes new alliances across age groups on the basis of common needs.

True <u>X</u> False ___

(M) 11. The growing federal and state allocations to programs for older adults have served to create a comprehensive and coordinated system of services accessible to older individuals.

      True ___   False _X_

(M) 12. Policy-making in the 1990s can be characterized as a process oriented to advancing efficiency and cost containment.

      True _X_   False ___

(C) 13. Recommendations from the Fourth White House Conference on Aging in 1995 emphasized enhancing Medicare and the Older Americans Act.

      True _X_   False ___

CHAPTER 16: HEALTH AND LONG-TERM CARE POLICY AND PROGRAMS

Glossary

Activities of Daily Living (ADL)

Capitated Payments

DRGs (Diagnostic Related Groupings)

Health Care Financing Administration

Health Maintenance Organizations (HMO)

Instrumental Activities of Daily Living (IADL)

Long-Term Care

Long-Term Care Insurance

Managed Care

Medicaid

Medicaid Waiver

Medical Savings Accounts

Medicare

Medicare Choices

On Lok

PACE

PPS (Prospective Payments)

Preferred Provider Organization

Propriety

Social Health Maintenance
  Organizations (SHMO)

Spend Down

Supplemental Security Income

Two-tier System of Health Care

Topics for Discussion

1.   The general public increasingly is concerned about the "crisis in health care," and policy-makers oftentimes blame the rapid growth of the older population for escalating costs in health and long-term care. What do you perceive to be the primary causes for these increasing costs? How would you respond to arguments that Medicare and Medicaid must be cut and consequently that benefits to older people must be limited?

2.   Describe the basic ways that long-term care services are organized and funded. What are the underlying assumptions and the consequences of these arrangements?

3.   What kinds of changes, if any, would you recommend in Medicare? In this discussion, consider the consequences of recent changes in Medicare, such as DRGs, increased co-payments, and cuts in payments to doctors, hospitals, and HMOs.

4.   What kinds of changes, if any, would you recommend in Medicaid?

5.   Presume that you are testifying before Congress on the need for long-term care reform. What would be the major components of your proposed reform with regard to older people?

6.   Describe the limitations of the growing number of private long-term care insurance schemes from the point of view of older people.

Multiple Choice

(E) 1. Medicare is designed to serve:

        a.   low-income older adults
        b.   institutionalized persons
        c.   older people with chronic disabilities
X   d.   all persons age 65 and over

(E) 2. A major problem with the current long-term health care system relative to older people is that it is:

        a.   oriented toward chronic conditions.
        b.   oriented toward home care.
        c.   oriented toward custodial care.
X   d.   oriented primarily toward acute care.

(E) 3. Which of the following is true of Medicaid?

        a.   It provides coverage for a limited amount of health services.
        b.   It offers basic hospital and optional supplementary insurance.
X   c.   It finances medical care primarily people receiving public assistance or SSI.
        d.   It covers medical care costs for people aged 65+ years of age, and for disabled Social Security beneficiaries.

(M) 4. Nursing home care is primarily financed by:

        a.   Supplemental Security Income
        b.   personal savings
X   c.   Medicaid
        d.   Medicare

(M) 5. In 1965, the new federal legislation establishing Medicare and Medicaid benefits signaled a philosophical change in the U.S. This new philosophy was that:

        a.   the federal government should establish a social welfare state
        b.   families should assume financial responsibility for their older members
X   c.   our society as a whole has a responsibility for older adults
        d.   none of the above

(M) 6. A fundamental assumption characterizing current long-term care services is:

        a. the public provision of services based on age and need
X   b. individuals are first responsible for the costs of long-term care
        c. the importance of curing disease
        d. none of the above

(C) 7. The primary factor underlying escalating health and long-term care costs is:

        a. more people reaching old age
        b. older people and their families are paying less for care
        c. older people's disproportionate utilization of hospital and physician services
X   d. inflation in hospital costs and physicians' fees and the growth of medical technology

(M) 8. Medicare covers the following health care costs:

        a. the full amount charged by health care providers
        b. prescription drugs
        c. dental care
        d. hearing and eye exams
X   e. none of the above

(C) 9. In an effort to control Medicare costs, the federal government has:

        a. offered incentives for preventive health care
        b. instituted co-payments and diagnostic related groupings
        c. increased the monthly premiums required for Part B
        d. none of the above
X   e. all of the above

(C) 10. Older people may qualify for Medicare if they:

        a. receive Supplemental Security Income (SSI)
        b. have high health care expenditures so that they "spend down"
        c. lack sufficient assets to cover Medicare's co-payments, deductibles, and monthly premiums
X   d. all of the above
        e. none of the above

(M) 11. Medicaid public expenditures have grown more rapidly than the federal inflation rate because:
    a.   Medicaid funds are administered by states
    b.   there has been a rapid increase in the number of Medicaid recipients
    c.   Medicaid recipients disproportionately utilize costly health services
X   d.   there have been substantial price increases charged by health care providers

(C) 12. Medicare part A (the Hospital Insurance Trust Fund) is predicted to be insolvent early in the 21st century largely because of:
X   a.   the changing age dependency ratio
    b.   it is financed on a yearly base and yearly income is declining
    c.   hospital and physician costs are escalating for the oldest-old
    d.   all of the above

(M) 13. "Medicare Choice", passed by Congress in 1997, encourages:

    a.   payment for a wider range of preventtive services
    b.   incentives for beneficiaries to use Health Maintenance Organizations
    c.   provisions for older people to establish their own Medical Savings Accounts
X   d.   all of the above
    e.   none of the above

(C) 14. Older people may be reluctant to apply for Medicaid because:

    a.   it can carry the stigma of welfare
    b.   some physicians are unwilling to treat Medicaid recipients
    c.   they will have fewer nursing home options open to them
    d.   they must first exhaust their own resources on medical expenses
X   e.   all of the above

(C) 15. Which of the following statements is true about the funding of the current long-term care system?

    a.   It provides an integrated and comprehensive system of both community-based and institutional options.
    b.   It finances an adequate level of home health care as a way to keep older people in their homes.
X   c.   It is dominated by institutional care.
    d.   It is guided by a national policy on long-term care.

(M) 16. A comprehensive system of long-term care should include:

    a.   health promotion and prevention of disease
    b.   respite and day care
    c.   home health care
    d.   institutional care, congregate care, and assisted living
X   e.   all of the above

(C)17. The need for publicly-funded home and community-based care services for older people is growing, because:

    a.   most older people prefer home care over hospital or nursing home care
    b.   since 1989, there has been more flexibility regarding the Medicare coverage for home care
    c.   growing numbers of older people require non-medical and personal care services
X   d.   all of the above
    e.   none of the above

(M) 18. Medicaid can be characterized by which of the following:

    a.   uniformity of benefits administered federally
X   b.   coverage of both skilled care for rehabilitation and for intermediate/custodial care in nursing homes
    c.   adequate coverage of personal care and home and community-based services
    d.   all of the above

(C) 19. Home care costs have grown dramatically in the past 10 years because of:

    a.   earlier hospital discharges have meant that more patients require more intensive technical care at home
    b.   an increase in the number of Medicare beneficiaries receiving home health services
    c.   an increase in for-profit home health agencies reimbursed under Medicare
X   d.   all of the above
    e.   none of the above

(C) 20. The way in which Medicaid is funded means that:

    a.   states must comply with federal regulations regarding which services to provide
X   b.   states can apply for waivers to provide community-based alternatives to institutionalization
    c.   most older people are covered by Medicaid
    d.   all of the above

(M) 21. As a whole, health and long-term care services for older people can be characterized by:

        a.   the growth of private insurance schemes that adequately fill the gaps left by public funding

X   b.   growing inequities and the creation of a two tier system of care

        c.   increasing emphasis upon the quality of care in hospitals and nursing homes

        d.   none of the above

(M) 22. Private long-term care insurance is characterized by:

        a.   adequate coverage for nursing home, home health and adult day care

        b.   reasonable costs for the average older adult

X   c.   inequities in coverage by race, gender and socioeconomic class

        d.   all of the above

(C)23. Health and long-term care reform has occurred:

        a.   primarily at the state level

        b.   through marketplace efforts to increase competitiveness and control costs

        c.   through managed care options such as HMO's and PPO's

X   d.   all of the above

        e.   none of the above

(C) 24. We can predict that federal health care legislation in the near future will be oriented toward:

        a.   expanding Medicare and Medicaid benefits for older people

        b.   increasing federal control of health care funding

X   c.   funding demonstration projects to integrate care and save costs

        d.   all of the above

True or False

(M) 1. Family caregivers of older adults primarily need increased Medicare/Medicaid funding
for   acute/short-term care.
> True ___   False _X_

(C) 2. Fee-for-service is a current health care reimbursement system whereby fees are
determined solely on the basis of diagnostic categories.
> True ___   False _X_

(E) 3. Medicare is given on the basis of age while Medicaid is given on the basis of financial
need.
> True _X_   False ___

(M) 4. A value underlying Medicare is that all older people are entitled to access to publicly
funded long-term care.
> True ___   False _X_

(M) 5. Long-term care refers to a broad range of care for chronic conditions.
> True _X_   False ___

(C) 6. The higher expenditures for health care for older people are due primarily to older
people's more frequent visits to doctors' offices and hospitals by the oldest-old segments
of our population.
> True ___   False _X_

(M) 7. Medicare and Medicaid are the fastest growing programs in the federal budget.

(M) 8. Older adults now spend a higher percentage of their income on acute health care
services than they did before the passage of Medicare.
> True _X_   False ___

(M) 9. A prospective payment system to limit payments in advance for a general course of
treatment applies to both Medicare-reimbursed home care and hospital care.
> True _X_   False ___

(C) 10. Older people are the primary users of Medicaid.
> True ___   False _X_

(E) 11. Fortunately, Medicare provides adequate health care protection for older Americans.
> True ___   False _X_

(M) 12. Because they want to avoid the stigma of Medicaid, most older nursing home residents are private pay   patients.

               True ___   False _X_

(M) 13. Private long-term care insurance is a recent development consistent with the philosophical assumptions underlying Medicare and Medicaid.

               True ___   False _X_

(C) 14. Changes in the prospective payment system have not yet reduced Medicare's overall costs.

               True _X_   False ___

(M) 15. The greatest gap in federal funding for long-term care is home and community-based care.

               True _X_   False ___

(C) 16. Lower income older people spend a higher proportion of their income on health care than do higher income elders.

               True _X_   False ___

(C) 17. The Social Services Block Grants and the Older Americans Act are able to cover most of the gaps in services left unfunded by Medicare and Medicaid.

               True ___   False _X_

EPILOGUE

Glossary

Social economic and demographic trends
Multigenerational families
Intergenerational relationships
  Vertical "beanpole" relationships
  Age-condensed family
  Truncated family
  "Women in the middle"
Reconstituted families
Work-retirement continuum
Cyclic life plans
Movement in and out of work force
"Third age"
Transitions to retirement
Phased retirement
Workplace modification
Job retraining

Productive aging
Successful aging
Integrating leisure across life span
Integrating technology into homes and caregiving
Long-term care
Managed care
Health maintenance organizations
Quality vs quantity of life
Telomerase
United Flying Octagenarians (UFO)

Topics for Discussion

1.   Discuss some potential outcomes of increased longevity with regard to family interactions and obligations. In what ways will changing attitudes toward divorce, remarriage, and women in the work force affect these relationships?

2.   Describe current patterns of retirement and how these may change with trends toward re-employment and retraining in some jobs.

3.   Discuss some technological advances that can empower older people and help them to live more independently. What are some of the limitations of these advances for older people?

4.   In what ways have hospitals and nursing homes begun to address the special needs of older patients? What other steps must acute and long-term care settings take to serve this growing population? What are some barriers to these changes?

5.   Describe the implications of increasing medical technology for bioethical issues related to the treatment of terminally ill older patients.

6.   Discuss future health and social service needs of the growing number of people with developmental disabilities living longer.

Multiple Choice

(M) 1. Demographic trends of the future suggest that people who are over age 65 in the 21st century:
- a. will comprise the majority of the population
- b. will be less educated than the current cohort of older adults
- X c. will have proportionately fewer young to take care of them
- d. will be more likely to rely on federal financial assistance

(M) 2. Increased opportunities for ethnic minorities and women today will result in:
- a. equality in earnings between white men and these other groups
- b. a greater proportion of ethnic minorities than whites among the future older population
- c. equal likelihood to suffer from cancer and heart disease as white men
- X d. slight improvements in the economic status of women and ethnic minorities

(M) 3. Changes in survival rates suggest that future older adults will:
- a. more likely live in 4-5 generational households
- X b. more likely be members of 4-5 generational families
- c. more likely have children and grandchildren caring for them
- d. have many members of step-families to care for them

(E) 4. Changes in fertility rates have resulted in a situation today in which:
- a. more adult children are available as caregivers for the aged
- X b. women can expect to spend more years caring for a parent than a child
- c. women can expect to spend more years caring for children than for parents
- d. fewer people will have grandparents surviving to old age

(M) 5. First time grandparenthood today generally occurs:
- a. at an earlier age
- b. at a later age
- X c. at a wide variety of ages from 35 to 75
- d. more often with step-grandchildren than with natural grandchildren

(M) 6. Differences in male and female longevity, as well as differences in attitudes about social networks, will result in:
- X a. more men relying on intragenerational ties
- b. more women turning to their sons for support
- c. more women living with their husbands in old age
- d. more men outliving their wives

(M) 7. Despite increasing life expectancy, married couples today are no more likely to reach their golden wedding anniversary than in the past because:

   X   a.   Divorce rates have increased.
           b.   Death rates among the old-old have not declined.
           c.   Marriage takes place much later today than in the past.
           d.   Life expectancy for older men has not improved.

(E) 8. The increased number of women in the workforce has resulted in the following changes in family caregiving responsibilities and services:

           a.   more men assuming caregiving roles
   X   b.   greater demands on women to provide caregiving in addition to working
           c.   increased support from the federal government for parental care
           d.   much more eldercare by grandchildren and great-grandchildren

(M) 9. Future cohorts of older persons will experience all of the following changes except:

           a.   more opportunities for job retraining
           b.   increased alternatives to full-time work after retiring
           c.   a greater proportion of their lives in retirement
   X   d.   very few people who need Social Security benefits

(M) 10. Changes in attitudes toward employment and retirement today will result in:

           a.   more people staying in their first jobs longer
   X   b.   increased numbers of adults seeking second and third careers
           c.   increased demands for technical education in high school
           d.   more people completing college by the age of 22

(M) 11. Future cohorts of older people will view leisure as:

           a.   a reward for many years of work
           b.   difficult to achieve because of demands for lifelong employment
   X   c.   a continuation of their lifestyles during their working years
           d.   something to avoid because it is contrary to the work ethic

(C) 12. The growth in computer technology suggests that future cohorts of older people will:

   X   a.   have the capability to be linked to the outside world even if they cannot leave their homes
           b.   be left behind in electronic communication because they are unfamiliar with computers
           c.   survive on their own with no input from their families
           d.   spend more for services and products advertised in the Internet

(M) 13. Baby boomers who become "senior boomers" will differ from earlier cohorts of older people in all of the following ways <u>except</u>?

    a.   They will be healthier and more oriented toward health promotion.
    b.   They will generally be financially better off.
    c.   They will be culturally and racially more diverse.
    d.   none of the above
X   e.   all of the above

(M) 14. Hospital care for older cohorts in the future will be characterized by which of the following?
    a.   less use of ambulatory services and more hospital days of care
    b.   greater competition for older patients
X   c.   more managed care and an emphasis on cost containment
    d.   more inpatient hospital care

(C) 15. The increase of the older population has raised numerous ethical issues because:

    a.   medical technology has made it possible to extended a healthy life, followed by a quick illness and death
    b.   the timing, place and conditions of death are increasingly under medical control.
X   c.   agreement does not exist about whether, how and under what circumstances to prolong life
    d.   medical technology has made it easier to draw a clear line between living and dying

(M) 16. The growth in geriatric training programs for many social and health service providers has all of the following implications <u>except</u>:

    a.   higher costs of care
    b.   greater options among
    c.   greater opportunity for interdisciplinary care
X   d.   lower costs of care

       True _____   False <u>X</u>

9.   A prospective payment system to limit payments in advance for a general course of treatment applies to both Medicare-reimbursed home care and hospital care.

       True <u>X</u>   False _____

(E) 1.   Future adults will be more likely to experience cyclical shifts between education, careers, and caregiving across the life span.
       True <u>X</u>   False _____

(E) 2.   By the year 2000, women and people of color will account for the majority of the labor force.
       True <u>X</u>   False _____

(M) 3.   There is a growing trend for older people to move to retirement apartments.
       True _____   False <u>X</u>

(E) 4.   The growth in home-based services and computers suggests that more of the future older population can remain in their own homes.
       True <u>X</u>   False _____

(M) 5.   The increased interest in "aging in place" has resulted in much more flexible housing design and options for older people today
       True _____   False <u>X</u>

(M) 6.   Ethical questions are increasing about the health care of older people largely because of diminishing resources and the increased costs of such care.
       True <u>X</u>   False _____

(E) 7.   The growth of subacute care units in many nursing homes has resulted in more beds available for Medicaid patients who need long-term care.
       True _____   False <u>X</u>

(M) 8.   Increased interest in complementary and alternative medicine by the public has led to more systematic research affecting older people.
       True <u>X</u>   False _____

(M) 9.   The increased number of trained geriatrics experts will probably result in higher health care costs for older people.
       True _____   False <u>X</u>

(M) 10. There is a growing emphasis on changing public policies to encourage older people to seek paid and unpaid work opportunities.

        True X   False _____

(E) 11. The verticalized or "beanpole" family structure refers to the fact that fewer family members are available within each generation to provide assistance to each other.

        True X   False _____

(M) 12. Fortunately, most corporations have now instituted programs to assist family members caring for older relatives.

        True _____   False X

(M) 13. Successful aging is equated with paid employment and work-oriented roles for older people.

        True _____   False X

(E) 14. The growth of medical technology has added to the problem of rationing health care.

        True X   False _____
        True X   False _____

(E) 15. Defining a situation as "medically futile", means that treatment offers no therapeutic benefit to a specific patient, not to all people with that condition.

        True X   False _____

(E) 16. Computer programs are now widely used by older people to obtain immediate medication reviews from their physicians.

        True _____   False X

1. NATIONAL ORGANIZATIONS AND AGENCIES RELATED TO AGING

ACTION - Older Americans Volunteer Programs, 1100 Vermont Avenue NW, Washington, DC 20525, (202) 634-9355.
http://www.cns.gov (corporation for national service)

A collection of national service organizations including the Senior Corp, which provide opportunity for people aged 55 and over to find local service opportunities related to their interests.

Administration on Aging (AOA), Department of Health and Human Services, 330 Independence Avenue SW, Washington, DC 20201, (202) 401-4634. (Office of the Assistant Secretary) Information available from the Executive Secretary, Harry Posman, Room 4757 at the above phone number.
http://www.aoa.dhhs.gov

The federal agency responsible for administering grant programs to the states. It is also a central source of information, technical assistance, and evaluation in the area of aging programs.

Alliance for Aging Research, Suite 305, 2021 K Street NW, Washington, DC 20006, (202) 293-2856.

This consumer group has free pamphlets like Improving Health with Antioxidants.

Alzheimer's Disease Education and Referral Center (ADEAR), PO Box 8250, Silver Springs, MD 20907-8250, (800) 438-4380.
http://www.alzheimers.org

A service of the National Institute on Aging (NIA), providing information about Alzheimer's disease, its impact on the family and health professional, and research into possible causes and cures.

Alzheimer's Disease and Related Disorders Association Inc. (ADRDA), 919 North Michigan Avenue, 10th floor, Chicago, IL 60611, (312) 335-8700.

Publishes Alzheimer's Disease and Related Disorders Newsletter, useful to both families and professionals. Provides research updates and news of Alzheimer's Support and Information Service Team chapters from around the country. Information packet available.

American Association for Geriatric Psychiatry, PO Box 376A, Greenbelt, MD 20768, (301) 220-0952.
http://www.aagpgpa.org/home/html

The AAGP is dedicated to improving the mental health and well-being of older people. AAGP's mission is to improve the knowledge base and standard of practice in geriatric psychiatry, and to be an active advocate for the nemtal health needs of a growing aging population.

American Association of Homes and Services for the Aging, 1129 20th Street NW, Suite 400, Washington, DC 20036-3489, (202) 296-5960.
http://www.aahsa.org

Members of this private nonprofit organization work with each other and the government in trying to identify and solve problems in homes for older people.

American Association of Retired Persons (AARP), 601 E Street NW, Washington, DC 20049, (202) 434-2300.
http://www.aarp.org

AARP works to meet the needs of older people throughout the nation. It offers a wide range of publications and services for persons over 55.

American College of Health Care Administrators (ACHCA), 325 South Patrick Street, Alexandria, VA 22314, (703) 739-7900.
http://www.achca.org

The professional society for over 6,000 administrators in long-term care, assisted living, and subacute care.

American Federation for Aging Research, 1414 Avenue of the Americas, 18th floor, New York, NY 10019, (212) 752-2327.
http://www.afar.org

This organization encourages and supports basic and clinical research in biomedical aspects of aging.

American Foundation for the Blind, Unit on Aging, 1660 L Street NW, Suite 214, Washington, DC 20036, (202) 467-5996, (800) 232-5463.
http://www.afb.org/specserv_age.html

A national clearinghouse for information about blindness and visual impairment. Updated list and designation of nationwide low-vision centers; series of self-help manuals; catalogues of low-vision aids, including clocks, watches, timers, games, medical aids, sewing and writing aids, tools, and measuring devices.

American Geriatrics Society Inc., 70 Lexington Avenue, Suite 300, New York, NY 10021, (212) 308-1414.
http://www.americangeriatrics.org

This organization emphasizes research and publication in the medical aspects of aging.

American Health Care Association, 1201 L Street NW, Washington, DC 20005, (202) 842-4444.
http://www.ahca.org

A federation of state associations of nursing homes. Publishes information on characteristics and status of profit and nonprofit homes.

American Medical Directors Association (AMDA), 10480 Little Patuxent Parkway, Suite 760, Columbia, MD 21044, (800) 876-AMDA.
http://www.amda.com

The national professional association for medical directors and physicians who practice in the long-term care continuum.

American Physical and Occupational Therapy Association, Section on Geriatrics, 1111 North Fairfax Street, Alexandria, VA 22314, (703) 706-3163 ext. 3237.
http://www.geriatricspt.org

A component of the American Physical Therapy Association comprised of over 7,000 physical therapists, students and physical therapy assistants committed to providing quality care for the geriatric client.

American Printing House for the Blind, 1839 Frankfort Avenue, PO Box 6085, Louisville KY 40206, (502) 895-2405.
http://www.aph.org

Catalogue of writing aids, tape recorders and educational materials.

American Public Welfare Association, 810 First Street NE, Suite 500, Washington, DC 20002-4267, (202) 682-0100.
http://www.apwa.org

Although not strictly devoted to the problems of aging, the APWA has published teaching materials for training in gerontology.

American Rehabilitation Association, formerly National Association of Rehabilitation Facilities, 1910 Association Drive, Suite 200, Reston, VA 22091, (703) 648-9300.

> An association of institutions and individuals that offer rehabilitation services, working to represent disabled persons interests to the Federal government.

American Seniors Housing Association, 1850 M Street NW, Suite 540, Washington, DC 20036, (202) 659-3381

> Provides technical guidance to a number of federal agencies on a variety of seniors' housing and long-term care issues.

American Society for Geriatric Dentistry, 211 East Chicago Avenue, Suite 948, Chicago, IL 60611, (312) 440-2660.
http://www.social.com:80/health/nhic/data/hr0300/hr0314.html

> The ASGD offers membership to dental professionals interested in clinical and research issues concerning the older adult. A monthly newsletter is published on relevant geriatric dental issues.

American Society for Long Term Care Nurses (ASLTCN/PADONA), 660 Lonely Cottage Drive, Upper Black Eddy, PA 18972, (610) 847-5396.
http://www.longtermcaretoday.com/asltcn.html

American Society on Aging, 833 Market Street, Suite 511, San Francisco, CA 94130, (415) 974-9600.
http://www.asaging.org

> National organization of educators, practitioners, and older people. Holds national and regional conferences. Publishes bimonthly newspaper, The Aging Connection, and journal Generations.

American Speech-Language Hearing Association, 10801 Rockville Pike, Dept. AP, Rockville, MD 20852, (301) 498-2071.
http://www.asha.org

> Can answer questions or mail information on hearing aids or hearing loss and communication problems in older people. Can also provide list of certified audiologists in each state.

Arthritis Foundation, 1330 West Peachtree Street, Atlanta, GA 30309, (404) 872-7100.
http://www.arthritis.org

> Publications available from the national office or from local chapters of the foundation.

Assisted Living Federation of America (ALFA), formerly Assisted Living Facilities Association of America, 10300 Easton Place, Suite 400, Fairfax, VA 22030, (703) 691-8100.
http://www.alfa.org

A trade association exclusively devoted to the assisted living industry and the population it serves. Members include assisted living providers as well as industry partners and supportive organizations.

Association for Gerontology in Higher Education (AGHE), 1001 Connecticut Avenue NW, Suite 400, Washington, DC 20036-5504, (202) 429-9277.
http://www.aghe.org

A national organization established to advance gerontology as a field of study in institutions of higher learning. Aims to foster research, instructional and service programs to enhance the capacities of institutions of higher education in the field of aging and to make their resources available to the wider community and society.

Association for Hospital Based Nursing Facilities (AHBNF), 3501 Mason's Mill Road, Suite 501, Huntington Valley, PA 19006, (215) 657-9992.

Better Hearing Institute, 5021-B Backlick Road, Annandale, VA 22003, (703) 642-0580, (1-800-EAR-WELL).
http://www.betterhearing.org

Maintains a toll-free Hearing Helpline that provides information about hearing aids, tinnitus, nerve deafness, special devices, and other problems related to hearing loss.

Caring Concepts, 793 Duncan Reidville Road, Duncan, SC 29334, 1-800-500-0260.
http://www.caringconcepts.com

Manufacturer of adaptive, assistive and traditional clothing for people with special needs.

Choice in Dying, National Office: 1035 - 30th Street NW, Washington, DC 20007, (202) 338-9790, Publications and Membership: 325 East Oliver Street, Baltimore, MD 21202, (410) 962-5454.

Formerly Concern for Dying and the Society for the Right to Die. Provides statutory advance directives and living wills for each state, free of charge, as well as other materials and services related to end-of-life medical care.

144

Citizens for the Improvement of Nursing Homes (CINH), 3530 StoneWay North, Seattle, WA 98103, (206) 461-4553.

A nonprofit statewide organization maintaining information on nursing homes, assisted living and adult family homes. Makes recommendations to persons seeking to place relatives.

Elder Care Locator, (800) 677-1116.

This national toll-free number is designed to help identify community resources for seniors anywhere in the United States. The name, address, and zip code of the person needing assistance allows the Elder Care Locator to identify the nearest information and assistance sources in that person's community. Call between 9:00 a.m. and 8:00 p.m. Eastern Time.

Elderhostel, 80 Boylston Street, Suite 400, Boston, MA 02116, (617) 426-8056. http://www.elderhostel.org

Offers educational opportunities through colleges nationwide and abroad.

Families USA, 1334 G Street NW, Washington, DC 20005, (202) 737-6340. http:///www.familiesUSA.org

A national nonprofit, non-partisan organization dedicated to high-quality, affordable health and long-term care for all Americans.

Family Caregiver Alliance, 425 Bush Street, Suite 500, San Francisco, CA 94108, (415) 434-3388.
http://www.caregiver.org/text/index.html

FCA is a nonprofit organization that assists family caregivers of adults suffering from memory loss as a result of chronic or progressive brain disorder. Its home page has much useful material for any caregiver, including individual fact sheets.

Federal Council on Aging, Room 4243 HHS North Building, 330 Independence Avenue SW, Washington, DC 20201, (202) 690-7525

A section of the Administration on Aging.

Foundation for Grandparenting, 7 Avenida Vista Grande, Suite B7-160, Santa Fe, New Mexico 87505,
http://www.grandparenting.org

A national organization that offers advice and assistance on grandparents' visitation rights.

Gatekeeper Program, Spokane Community Mental Health Center Elderly Services, South 107 Division, Spokane, WA 99202, (509) 838-4651.

This program utilizes non-traditional referral sources who come into contact with high-risk older individuals. They offer training videos, training manuals, and other material relative to the concept of active case finding and in-home delivery systems.

Generations United, 440 First Street NW, Suite 310, Washington, DC 20001-2085, (202) 942-0315
http://www.gu.org

Seeks to foster intergenerational activities.

Geriatric Video Productions Inc., PO Box 1757, Shavertown, PA 18708, 1-800-621-9181.
http://www.geriatricvideo.com

An educational video production company specializing in programs in geriatric nursing that improve geriatric nursing skills and contribute to improved patient outcomes.

Gerontological Society of America, 1275 K Street NW, Suite 350, Washington, DC 20005-4006, (202) 842-1275.
http://www.geron.org

A professional organization devoted to the research, publication, and exchange of information on aging. The society also sponsors an annual conference, and publishes three journals; The Gerontologist, Journal of Gerontolotgy-Series A, and Series B.

Gray Panthers, 2025 Pennsylvania Avenue NW, Suite 821, Washington, DC 20006, (202) 466-3132. *(in the process of developing a national web page)*
http://www.igc.apc.org/graypantherssf

National intergenerational activist movement concerned with eradication of ageism. The Panthers hold conferences and workshops, maintain a speakers' bureau, and help groups organize.

Hemlock Society, PO Box 101810, Denver Colorado 80250-1810, 1-800-247-7421.
http://www.hemlock.org/hemlock

A program of education, research, and advocacy to encourage public acceptance of legal voluntary physician aid-in-dying for terminally ill, mentally competent adults.

Hospice Association of America, 228 7th Street SE, Washington, DC 20003, (202) 546-4759.
http://www.nahc.org/HAA

> HAA is a national organization representing hospices, caregivers and volunteers who serve terminally ill patients and their families. HAA is the largest lobbying group for hospice, advocating the industry's interest before Congress, regulatory agencies and other national organizations.

International Federation on Aging, 601 E Street NW, Washington, DC 20049, (202) 434-2430.

> A private nonprofit organization linking approximately 100 associations that represent or serve older persons at the grassroots level in 50 nations around the world.

International Hearing Aid Helpline, 16880 Middlebelt Road, Livonia, MI 48152, (800) 521-5247.
http://www.ihshearing.org

> Provides information on hearing aids and distributes a listing of hearing aid specialists certified by the International Hearing Society.

Library of Congress, Blind and Physically Handicapped Division, 1291 Taylor Street NW, Washington, DC 20542, (202) 707-5104.
http://lcweb.loc.gov

> Resource for talking books for the visually impaired.

Long Term Acute Care Hospital Association of America (LTACHAA), 1301 K Street NW, Suite 1100, East Tower, Washington, DC 20005, (202) 296-4446.

> Lobbies to preserve Medicare exemptions for long-term acute care hospitals.

National Academy on an Aging Society, 1275 K Street, Suite 350, Washington, DC 20005-4006, (202) 408-3375.

> Seeks to encourage innovative and responsible thinking on critical aging policy issues. Such issues include health care, long term care and income security in interactional context.

National Adult Day Services Association, NCOA, 409 3rd Street SW, 2nd Floor, Washington, DC 20024, (202) 479-6682.

> Part of the National Council on Aging, this organization represents interests of adult day providers throughout the U.S.

National Alliance for Caregiving, 4720 Montgomery Lane, Bethesda, MD 20814-3425 (3010 718-8444.

A nonprofit venture of several national organizations aiming to focus attention on family caregiving through research, program development and public awareness activities.

National Asian Pacific Center on Aging, Melbourne Tower, Suite 914, 1511 Third Avenue, Seattle, WA 98101, (206) 624-1221.
http://www.NAPCA.org (web page currently under construction)

The only national organization serving all segments of the older Asian Pacific Islanders (API) population, including Chinese, Japanese, Korean, Filipino, Lao, Cambodian, Vietnamese, Malayan, and Pacific Islanders. Its mission is to be the unified voice for API elders throughout the U.S., and to promote and provide programs that enhance the dignity and quality of life for API elders.

National Association for Continence, PO Box 8310, Spartanburg, SC 29303, (864) 579-7900, or 1-800-252-3337.
http://www.nafc.org

A clearinghouse for educational materials on incontinence - leaflets, books and videos. Also provides a referral service to local medical and nursing specialists on incontinence, including information on professionals' education and experience.

National Association for Hispanic Elderly , 234 East Colorado Blvd., Suite 300, Pasadena, CA91101, (626) 564-1988.

Provides social services and employment programs for low-income Hispanic elderly. Offers information and referral for SSI eligibility. Produces documentaries and public service announcements.

National Association for Home Care (NAHC), 228 7th Street SE, Washington, DC 20003, (202) 547-7424.
http://www.nahc.org

NAHC monitors federal and state activities affecting home care and focuses on issues relating to home health care. They publish the magazine Caring on a bimonthly basis.

National Association of Area Agencies on Aging, 1112 16th Street NW, Suite 100, Washington, DC 20036, (202) 296-8130.
http://www.n4a.org

Functions in agreement with the US Administration on Aging to assist older Americans to stay in their own homes and communities with maximum independence. Operates the Eldercare Locator (see above) and publishes the National Directory for Eldercare.

National Association of Directors of Nursing in Long Term Care (NADONA/LTC), 10999 Reed Hartman Hwy, Suite 229, Cincinnati, OH 45242-8301, (800) 222-0539. http://www.nadona.org

A professional non-profit association specifically serving Directors and Assistant Directors in nursing in long-term care. Promotes quality of care for long term care residents and establishes Standards of Practice for Directors of Nursing in long term care.

National Association of Nutrition and Aging Services Programs, 2675 44th Street SW, Suite 305, Grand Rapids, MI 49509, (616) 531-8700. http://www.aoa.shhs.gov/aoa/dir/nanasp.html

A professional membership organization representing nutrition and other home and community based providers serving older and disabled adults across the United States.

National Association of Residential Care Facilities (NARCF), 11480 Sunset Hill Road, Reston, VA 22091, (703) 709-7850. http://www.health-connect.com/nacrf/

A national, non-profit trade association whose members primarily serve the long-term needs of frail older adults, mentally and / or physically impaired, and developmentally disabled.

National Association of Retired Federal Employees, 606 North Washington Street, Alexandria, VA 22314-1914, (703) 838-7760. http://www.narfe.org

National organization which represents the interests of retired federal employees. Publishes a monthly magazine and offers special life, health, and auto insurance rates.

National Caucus and Center on Black Aged, 1447 Peachtree Street, Suite 1003, Atlanta, GA 30309, (404) 892-6222.

An advocate organization working on behalf of the black elders. Publishes a newsletter, conducts research, and disseminates information on aging and aged blacks. An equal opportunity organization that helps all older ethnic minorities find employment.

National Center on Elder Abuse, (202) 682-2470.

Funded by the Administration of Aging as an information clearinghouse.

National Citizen's Coalition for Nursing Home Reform (NCCNHR), 1424 16th Street NW, Suite 202, Washington, DC 20036, (202) 332-2275.

A private citizens' group focused on improving quality of nursing homes nationwide, and the quality of residents' lives.

National Clearinghouse on Aging, Administration on Aging, OHD/DHHS, 330 Independence Avenue SW, Washington, DC 20201, (202) 401-4634.

Federal office responsible for collecting, analyzing and disseminating information about aging and aging program.

National Coalition of Grandparents (NCOG), 137 Larkin, Madison, WI 53705, (608) 238-8751.

Works toward legislative changes to ensure a child's right to a safe, stable environment and to strengthen intergenerational family bonds.

National Committee to Preserve Social Security and Medicare, #10 G Street NE, Suite 600, Washington, DC 20002, (202) 216-0420.

Publishes Viewpoint, an analysis of current legislation and the committee's recommended action.

National Council of Senior Citizens (NCSC), 8403 Colesville Road, Suite 1200, Silver Spring, MD 20910, (301) 578-8800.
http://www.ncscinc.org

NCSC is composed of representatives of seniors' organizations throughout the nation. Its foci are on education and social action.

National Council on Patient Information and Education (NCPIE), 666 11th Street NW, Suite 810, Washington, DC 20001, (202) 347-6711.
http://www.aoa.dhhs.gov/aoa/dir/151.html

A cooperative effort of the National Institute on Aging and the Administration on Aging, the National Council on Patient Information and Education is committed to improving communication between health care professionals and patients about prescription medicines.

National Council on the Aging Inc. (NCOA), 409 third Street SW, Suite 200, Washington, DC 20024, (202) 479-1200.
http://www.ncoa.org

A private, nonprofit corporation which serves as a central resource for information, technical assistance, training, planning and consultation in gerontology.

National Family Caregivers Association, 9621 East Bexhill Drive, Kensington, MD 20895-3650, (200) 896-3650.
http://www.nfacares.org

NFCA is a national nonprofit membership organization. Members can receive service and products including a 12 page newsletter, "Take Care! Self-Care for the Family Caregiver".

National Hospice Organization (NHO), 1901 North Fort Moore Drive, Suite 901, Arlington, VA 22209, (703) 243-5900.
http://www.nho.org

A national organization that works to educate about and advocate for the philosophy of hospice care to meet the unique needs of each terminally ill person and his or her family.

National Indian Council on Aging, City Center, Suite 510W, 6400 Uptown Blvd. NE, Albuquerque, NM 87110, (505) 292-2001.
http://www.aoa.dhhs.gov/aoa/dir/160.html

Endeavors to improve the lives of Indian and Alaskan Native elders through specialized activities. Maintains a cooperative relationship with a number of federal agencies, conducting research on aging and issuing reports on the needs of Indian and Alaskan native elders.

National Institute of Neurological Disorders and Stroke, PO Box 5801, Bethesda, MD 20824, (301) 496-5751.
http://www.ninds.nih.gov

This institute offers information and publications on disorders such as dementia, stroke, brain tumors, and Parkinson's disease.

National Institute on Adult Day Care, 6000 Maryland Avenue SW, West Wing 100, Washington, DC 20024, (800) 424-9046.

Publishes a directory of adult day care in the United States. Ask for order #2022.

National Institute on Aging (NIA), Building 31, Room 5C27, 31 Center Drive, Bethesda, MD 20892, (301) 496-1752.
http://www.nih.gov/nia

Part of the National Institutes of Health. Funds scientific research on basic mechanisms of aging and diseases related to aging, as well as behavioral and clinical studies of aging.

National Osteoporosis Foundation, 1150 17th Street NW, Suite 500, Washington, DC 20036, (202) 223-2226.
http://www.nof.org

Provides information on osteoporosis diagnosis, treatment and prevention.

National Policy and Resource Center on Women and Aging, C/O Heller School, MS 035, Brandeis University, Waltham, MA 02254-9110.

Publishes a quarterly newsletter, Women and Aging, conducts research and sponsors conferences on women.

National Senior Citizens' Law Center, 1101 14th Street NW, Suite 400, Washington, DC 20005, (202) 289-6979.
http://www.nsclc.org

A central national resource for legal services programs serving low income older people: works at federal, state, and local levels to see that needs of low income older people are met.

National Shared Housing Resource Center, 431 Pine Street, Burlington, VT 05401, (802) 862-2727.

.The center publishes a pamphlet, Is Homesharing for You? A Self-Help Guide for Homeowners and Renters. They also serve as a resource center and offer technical assistance for 350 shared housing projects nationally.

Network News: A Newsletter of the Global Link for Midlife and Older Women, 601 E Street NW, Washington, DC 20049, (202) 4334-2300.
http://www.aarp.org

Sponsored by AARP in cooperation with the International Federation on Aging.

Older Women's League, 666 Eleventh Street NW, Suite 700, Washington, DC 20001, (202) 783-6686, 1-800-TAKE-OWL.
http://www.womenconnect.com/organizations/or20550h.htm

National advocacy and educational organization. Focuses on issues of economic security, health care and caregiving.

Raising Our Children's Kids: An Intergenerational Network of Grandparenting, Inc. (ROCKING), PO Box 96, Niles, MI 49120, (616) 683-9038.

Maintains a directory of support groups for caregivers by each state. Now seeking the passage of a mandated kinship care program in all 50 states.

SAGE: Senior Action in a Gay Environment, 305 7th Avenue, 16th floor, New York, NY, 10001, (212) 741-2247.

Newsletter and resource directory about groups providing services to older gay men and lesbians.

Self-Help for Hard of Hearing People (SHHH), 7910 Woodmont Avenue, Suite 1200, Bethesda, MD 20814, (301) 657-2248.
http://www.shhh.org

SHHH is a nationwide organization for the hard of hearing. Publishes a bimonthly journal reporting the experiences of those with hearing impairments as well as new developments in the field of hearing loss.

US Department of Commerce--Social and Economics Statistics Administration, Bureau of the Census, Washington, DC 20233, (202) 763-5190.
http://www.doc.gov (census is http://www.census.gov)

This agency publishes the "Current Population Reports" which include population, income, education, housing, etc. data.

US Senate Special Committee on Aging, G31 Dirksen Senate Office Building, Washington, DC 20510-6400, (202) 224-5364.
http://www.senate.gov/comm/aging/general

2. ADDITIONAL WEBSITES RELATED TO AGING

AgeNet, LLC, 644-A West Washington Avenue, Madison, WI 53703, (608) 256-4242.
http://www.agenet.com

> An information and referral network designed to communicate information about products and services that are important to enhancing the quality of life of older adults and their families.

Caregiving
http://www.caregiving.com

> A webpage and monthly newsletter tailored to the caregiver of an aging friend or relative.

Eldercare Web
http://www.elderweb.com

> A collection of links and resources pertaining to care of the physical, social, and mental needs of frail elders.

"Growing Old in a New Age": Telecourse on social gerontology, linked to this textbook.
http://www2.hasaii.edu/sphcoa

> Developed as an international meeting place for instructors, students, community agencies, corporations and individuals/families who are using the telecourse.

G-NEURO

> This email discussion group emphasizes neurobehavioral disorders relating to older adults. To subscribe, send a message to LISTSERV@SJUVM.STJOHNS.EDU. Leave the subject line blank, and send the one-line message: subscribe G-NEURO (your firstname, lastname).

Medical Matrix: Geriatrics
http://www.medmatrix.org/index/asp

> This site has links to many of the best Internet resources on geriatrics, including a "News" section with direct links to full text articles on aging published by the New York Times Syndicate.

MedWeb: Geriatrics
http://www.gen.emory.edu/medweb.geriatrics.html

> Includes direct links to hundreds of sites dealing with specific problems of aging.

Resources for Senior Citizens
http://www.bev.net/community/seniors/Seniors.html

A nonprofit project providing seniors with "a national online network, locally sponsored and operated learning centers, and educational publications".

3. Periodicals

Age Page. Published by the National Institute on Aging, PO Box 8057, Gaithersburg, MD 20898-8057, (800) 222-2225.

AARP Highlights. Published by AARP, 1909 K Street NW, Washington, DC 20049.

Aging. Published by the Administration on Aging, Washington, DC 20201. Available from Superintendent of Documents Department of Health and Human Services, 200 Independence Avenue SW, Washington, DC 20201, (202) 245-6296, $15.

Ageing and Society. Cambridge University Press, Journals Department, 40 West 20th Street, New York, NY 10011-4211, (212) 924-3900.
http://www.journals.cup.org

American Journal of Alzheimer's Disease. 470 Boston Post Road, Weston, MA 02193, (781) 899-2707.
http://www.alzheirmersjournal.com

American Journal of Geriatric Psychiatry.
http://www.appi.org/ajgptoc.html

Archives of Gerontology and Geriatrics.
http://www.elsevier.nl:80/esstoc/publications/store/3/01674943/

Clinical Gerontologist. The Haworth Press, Inc., 10 Alice Street Brighamton, NY 13904-7981, (800) 895-0582.
http://www.haworth.com

Collation. National Citizens' Coalition for Nursing Home Reform, 1424 16th Street NW, Washington, DC 20036, (202) 797-0657.

Generations. 833 Market Street, Suite 511, San Francisco, CA 94103-1824, (415) 974-9644. Published by the American Society on Aging.

Geriatric Medicine.
http://www.docnet.org.uk

Geriatrics. Edgell Communications, 7500 Old Oak Blvd., Cleveland, OH 44130.

Geriatrics: Medicine for Midlife and Beyond.
http://www.modernmedicine.com/geri/

International Journal of Aging and Human Development. Baywood Publishing Co. Inc., 26 Austin Avenue, PO Box 337, Amityville, NY 11701.

Journal of Adult Development. Plenum Publishing Corp., 233 Spring Street, New York, NY 10013, (212) 620-8468.

Journal of Aging and Social Policy. The Haworth Press Inc., 10 Alice Street, Brignamton, NY 13904-7981, (800) 429-6784.
Http://www.haworth.com

Journal of Aging Studies. JAI Press Inc., 55 Old Post Road #2, PO Box 1678, Greenwich, CT 06836-1678.

Journal of the American Geriatrics Society.
http://www.wwilkins.com/AGD/

Journal of Applied Gerontology. Center for Gerontology, Virginia Polytechnic Institute and State University, 237 Wallace Hall, Blacksburg, VA 24061-0426.

Journal of Gerontological Social Work. The Haworth Press, 12 West 32nd Street, New York, NY 10001.

Parenting Grandchildren: A Voice of Grandparents. AARP, Grandparent Information Center, 601 E Street NW, Washington, DC 20049.

Resources for the Aging: an Action Handbook. Published by NCOA, 600 Maryland Avenue SW, West Wing 100, Washington, DC 20024. Prepared for OEO, second edition (202) 479-1200.

Seniority. Published by the National Council of Senior Citizens Inc., 8403 Colesville Road, Suite 1200, Silver Spring, MD 20910-3314, (301) 578-8800.

US Senate Special Committee on Aging Memorandum. Published by the US Senate Special Committee on Aging, SD-G31, Senate Office Building, Washington, DC 20510-6400. Published several times monthly.